Wand and Weaver

Book 1

The Chain

By C. E. Dorsett

The Chain

Wand and Weaver: Book 1

For more information and more Titles, please visit:

dashPunk.com
DragonsOfNight.com
WandAndWeaver.com

Thanks to

Our Beta Readers:
Chris, John, Kathy, and Mable

My Inspiration:
For all those who struggle to live a life they love in a world of lies and pain. Hope and love will get us through. The shadows always pass.

Table of Contents

Chapter 1

Plan B

Nathan waved his hand in front of the mirror on his little desk. He poured his emotions down his arm, through his fingertips into the polished glass. He needed to see a friendly face.

His little room was dark, a solitary table candle carrying light and his prayers into the cold.

Again, he focused a call to Rouge through the mirror. This time, he allowed his urgency and pain to flow into the glass.

The image shimmered. His creamy pale face and short reddish brown hair faded, replaced by Rouge's tussled black mane and angular features. His heart wavered for a moment and the image faded, then returned.

"Nathan?" Rouge said, surprised by the call. The image shook a bit. He must be using a pocket mirror.

"Yeah," Nathan grabbed the tears before they could escape his eyes and forced the emotion into the call. "I'm coming home."

Rouge fell back into what must have been a chair and the image twisted into an old wooden ceiling lit by a small lamp then back to Rouge's face. "What happened?"

"At least the old man hasn't called out the pitchforks and torches, yet."

Rouge raised an eyebrow, "Did you spill water on him or forget to wear white?"

"Be serious, I gave a sermon this morning, and the Herald, in his infinite wisdom," he tried to keep the hate out of his voice, but the wound was still raw. He closed his eyes, and inhaled slowly. Forcing a smile on his face, "He didn't like it when I said our separation from the non-magical world didn't necessarily mean total isolation and rejection of everything outside the community." Nathan's lips quivered.

He opened his eyes, tears welled up, and moved down his face like a funeral procession. They carried his dreams with them. He was expelled from seminary. He could never be a curate— never serve his people or his ancestors upholding the covenant with the Giants. His fifteen minute sermonette burned that bridge.

"Sweetie," Rouge's concern reached out and touched Nathan's heart. "I don't understand. What was wrong with saying that?"

Nathan shrugged and shook his head so slow he felt time grinding to a halt. "I didn't say anything new or novel." He choked on his sorrow, the loss set in. "I quoted the elders to make my points. None of that mattered. The congregation applauded, then Herald Paul Kincaid," contempt filled his voice again, "Leapt to his feet and shouted, Blasphemy! Your words not only endanger you but endanger the whole Sith Thyrsa. Hie folgiath se sith thara thyrsa!"

Hie folgiath se sith thara thyrsa. The ancient creed echoed through Nathan's head. We follow the path of the Giants. With one simple proclamation in Old English, the Herald accused him of spitting on the graves of his ancestors, defying the will of the Giants, and breaking the covenant.

Nathan could still hear the words, feel the heat, the brand of disapproval. He wanted to grow cold. "The congregation repeated the creed and turned against me." He couldn't hold it in any longer. He wept. He tried to keep talking, but his words were punctuated by breathy sobs. "He had me," pain wracked his soul, "ushered out of the shrine," he shook his head back and forth like he was trying to erase the event from history, "To my room in the abbey and told me to pack." He looked into Rouge's pained face in the glass.

"That's bullshit!" Rouge snarled.

Nodding, Nathan wiped the tears from his face, and drew on every bit of strength he had left. "I don't have a lot of time. I need you to do somethings for me. I can't come home in full disgrace."

"Anything for you, you know that," Rouge touched the mirror.

"Your name is still on my accounts. Take the money I have in there and rent us a house."

The image on the mirror rocked around as Rouge set it down on a table and adjusted it. He picked up a pen and paper, and started writing.

"And remember that Fetehouse we used to talk about starting?" Nathan asked.

Rouge's eyes lit up.

"Are you still interested?" Nathan held his breath,

Rouge nodded wildly, "We desperately need one in the area."

"Find a place, rent it, and get hold of Robin." Nathan forced himself to smile. "Let's do it!"

Nathan took his right hand off the wheel of his burgundy Stirling Regen and tapped the quartz crystal inlaid in the dashboard.

"Soothing music," he said.

The car responded. Blackmoore's Night started playing. He didn't pay attention to which song. He would be at the 26 exit soon. His mind raced.

How was he going to explain to his parents in Schleyfield why he was back in Maryland so soon? He could tell them the truth.

"Mom, Dad, I pissed off the Herald of Philadelphia by speaking out publicly against his anti-wrecca teaching," he mumbled under his breath, then sighed. "Yeah, that will go over really well." He sighed again.

He took the exit to go east on 26. Traffic was thick. It would take some time to get to the bridge. He stayed in the far right lane.

Nathan drove on, not far from home now. How could he face his family? He took a couple days to come home, staying with a friend in Philadelphia. That gave Rouge enough time to put the pieces in place. The plan would work. He returned for an opportunity. That was true, even if not the whole truth. Nathan saw the bridge over the Monocacy River coming up.

"Moura, acythe thaet infaer!" He waved his hand toward the right side of the road. The shoulder rippled and an exit appeared just to him. None of the other motorists could see it.

Turning off 26, he pulled up to the river, and stopped the car near the bank.

The Monocacy never looked threatening to him before. He and Rouge used to play along the bank, and swim all summer. Robin taught them how to catch brownies and hobs here. He loved the river.

Now, it was the only thing keeping him from facing his friends and family. Once he crossed the river, he would see their disappointment.

He looked up at the trees. The branches tossed in the breeze, reflecting the sunlight into his eyes. He wanted to see them as the welcoming branches they always used to be. Nothing changed about the trees. Something was different about him.

The water rose up from the center of the river to greet him. Light cascaded as if through crystal, forming a beautiful, young woman with long, flowing, gold hair.

He stopped the motor, and slowly stepped out of the car. The cool December air pricked his skin. An icy breeze gushed from the Moura. Nathan bowed his head to her.

"Hello, drymann," she said in a seductive voice, "I have been waiting for you to return."

Nathan smirked. "I know, returning in shame, just open the road."

The Moura stepped out of the river, shaking her head. "Now is that how you want to pass by, with a shadow in your heart?"

"How else?" he closed the car door to stop too much cold air from getting in. "I left to become a curate, and I was expelled. They will call me a failure. Might as well get ready."

The Moura smiled, "I heard. The Herald himself asked me to keep an eye on you. Are you a threat?"

"No!" Nathan squared his jaw.

"But you carry the guilt in your heart," the Moura closed her eyes, "Yes, you carry the guilt and doubt deep within. I am suppose to keep the town safe. How can I let you through when a Herald thinks you might be dangerous, and you are afraid he might be right?"

Nathan watched the sun glimmer on the surface of the water. She had a point. "Moura, may I ask you a question?"

She nodded.

Nathan took in a deep breath, "If I were the threat the Herald thought I was, would they have allowed me to leave the Abbey?"

The Moura smiled. "No. They would have turned you over to the authorities and charged you with violating the covenant."

"Then I must not be that much of a threat."

The Moura's smile broadened, "You haven't changed at all," she laughed, "I will send word ahead to your parents."

Nathan quickly opened the car door and dove inside.

The Moura turned to the river and folding her hands together over her head, leapt into the air. Water splashed from the river. The air ripped open under her like unzipping a zipper. The opening widened until the road was clear and the multicolored brick building of Schleyfield came into view.

Home, Nathan smiled.

Nathan took a deep breath and started the car, and pulled through the curtain of water. He wended around the streets for a while emerging from the far side of town, then out into the countryside for a bit until the golden brick of his parents' house loomed on the hill.

He didn't know how they would react, but he braced himself for the worst. He pulled into his parent's driveway, "It's showtime."

Nathan sat in his car. Pulling down the sun visor, his emerald eyes were stained red from crying on the drive home. His reddish brown hair defiantly stood up in odd places.

The storm door to his Parent's House opened and squeaked closed. He didn't want to look. He knew his mother's eyes would overflow with disappointment, and he wasn't sure if he could handle seeing that.

Stepping out of his little Regen, he made himself to look at the porch.

His mother forced a smile across her disappointment. Frowning wore deep grooves around her mouth and eyes.

"I was shocked when the Moura said you were on your way," she said.

Nathan knew that tone of voice. She was really asking, "Why aren't you still at the abbey?"

She didn't know. If Nathan wanted to he could cover up what happened. He weighed the pros and cons of telling her the truth or concocting a lie. He decided to try an omission.

"I was talking to Rouge, and came back to work on something with him." It was half true.

She shook her head and pursed her lips to the point they nearly disappeared. "You left the Abbey for a project."

"It was a good opportunity." He smiled as best he could. "I really missed everyone and thought, why not?"

His mother turned around and put her hand on the door, "Your father should be home soon. I just washed some ten-toed squash I'd been saving. Come on in." Without a pause she opened the door and went in.

Evelyn Kell was a strong woman. She'd practically raised her sisters. She was set in her ways and suspicious of everything. She'd had a hard life before she met Creed Kell, and wore the battle scars on her sleeves.

Nathan was her youngest son, the youngest of four children. She expected a lot from all of them, but she had her highest hopes for Nathan.

Now, he had disappointed her like so many others. He ambled toward the door. He didn't know what to expect inside. She would already be in the kitchen cooking.

The intoxicating aroma of his mother's chicken fried steak greeted him in the living room. The house looked like it always did. The floors were spotless, and every surface was covered with decorations, papers, magazines, and books.

He walked into the kitchen, and saw his mother standing at the stove monitoring several pans and skillets.

"I called your sisters and brother and told them you were home. Cara said she would be right over."

Nathan nodded. Cara would come, but Ian and Didi were probably busy. They always had something else to do. They couldn't even manage the time to visit Grandpa Kell in the hospital before he died.

"So, Nathan," Evelyn continued, "What was so important that you left the Abbey?"

"I came back to start a Fetehouse with Rouge," Nathan said, watching her back stiffen. "We talked about it before I left, and I thought Grandpa's money would go to better use helping the community."

"You have always been a bit of a dreamer," her voice sounded like tears. "You realize what a gamble this is right? Bars usually go out of business their first year."

Nathan looked down at the faux-stone floor. He traced the grooves with his eyes for a moment. "I have enough to float us at least that long. He found a building on Fritchie Road. It is perfect."

She didn't turn around, didn't look at him. "Be more realistic. That money was your grandfather's legacy. You don't need to buy yourself a playhouse so you and your friends can play dress up."

"Do you really think that is what this is all about?" Nathan almost choked on the words. "There is so much more to it than just dressing up!"

His mother sighed. "You just need to learn how to dream smaller, and to get in touch with real life. It is not all fun and games."

He wanted to scream, "I know that!" but didn't. He wondered if she ever realized how her words hurt him, cutting him like a knife thrust into his soul.

"You were always a dreamer," she continued, "In school, you always had a plan. When they fell apart it was never your fault. Life is not that easy."

She was right. His encounter with Herald Kincaid blocked him from his dream of joining the curate. He blamed Paul, but it was really his fault. Sometimes life was that simple.

He turned around, and marched back out into the cold.

Nathan stood on the porch of his parent's house looking north, toward Pennsylvania, toward his Waterloo. This was why he didn't tell her the whole truth. She would find out in time, but for now, this was enough for her to worry about.

He heard a car in the driveway, and looked over. His sister, Cara's, black Sterling Bohemian pulled in.

As she exited the car, Nathan smiled and ran to give her a hug. They embraced, and just for a moment all the problems went away.

"I love that suede coat," Nathan said, "Is that new?"

Cara nodded and brushed her brown hair out of her face, "What are you doing back so soon?"

"I came back to start a Fetehouse with Rouge," Nathan answered.

She looked him up and down, "They kicked you out, didn't they?"

"What?" Nathan took a small step back, "No."

Cara looked over her glasses at him, "What did you do?"

"I don't know what you are talking about."

Cara laughed, "You could never lie to me. So you told mom you came back for the Fetehouse, what really happened?"

Nathan looked around to make sure his mother wasn't in earshot. "Herald Kincaid accused me of heresy for not hating non-magical people."

Cara squinted, "That isn't heresy. Father Hugh always said we are suppose to love the wrecca. We separate ourselves from them to protect ourselves from their jealousy and fear."

Nathan leaned up against the car, "And that is all I said... Something is wrong. They didn't exile us, we exiled them. They are the wrecca."

"Something doesn't sit right with me," Cara shook her head, "Why would the Herald be so upset about that? There has to be something else."

"All I said is that separation is not that same as isolation." Nathan ran over the words of his sermonette in his head. "I cited the founders, Fritha, Scildend, and Creoda. I even quoted the Sith Thyrsa they wrote."

"Do you think Creoda has decided that he wants the throne of England again?" Cara leaned on the car next to her brother.

Nathan's heart froze. "I hope not! That would break the covenant. We would lose everything. . ." Images of the witch trials flooded his mind.

"So, how much of a reality is this Fetehouse?" Cara broke the awkward silence.

"A big one. Rouge rented out 1334 Fritchie Road. We are going to call it, Wand and Weaver. The sign is already being made."

"Well, if you have a sign," Cara laughed. "I'm sure mom accused you of wanting to play dress up."

Nathan nodded.

"You have it all worked out?" She looked over at him, "This isn't just a new club house, right? I mean, last time we saw Mira, it was you looking for a bit of acceptance. I wondered if you joined the curate because mom didn't approve of the whole thing."

"Seriously?" Nathan took a couple steps away from the car and faced his sister. "I have always had these two parts of me, and now is Mira's time."

"You know, if you would just settle down with the right man, someone who loved you for you, then maybe you wouldn't feel the need to dress up."

"You just don't understand." Nathan huffed. "This household never accepted me for all that I am."

Cara narrowed her eyes, "How long are you going to give Wand and Weaver to take off before you get a real job?"

Nathan gawked at her for a moment. He couldn't believe she just said that. "Wand and Weaver is going to work!" he said, "You'll see! I am not the looser you all seem to think I am!"

Their father arrived in his Mithras truck, and they postponed the argument.

Creed welcomed his son with a simple greeting. He was a man of few words, a tradesman whose face was prematurely aged and weathered by a life of physical labor. He walked with a slight limp, but always had a smile on his face.

The three of them went inside.

Evelyn had already set the table, and they ate in relative silence: chicken fried steak; buttered ten-toed squash; green beans, okra, and potatoes boiled with onions and bacon; and stovetop cornbread. The food was divine as always.

After eating, Creed turned on the Broadview scrying crystal and started watching a show about the Outland Caravans.

Cara and Evelyn talked about the new house she and her husband just moved into.

Nathan realized he was no longer necessary to the conversation, and excused himself. It was time to go to his new home.

He walked as fast as he could through the cold night air to get in the car and turn on the heat. He pulled out and drove toward town for a while before turning off on Vale Wry Drive toward the house he had been paying for Rouge to live in.

Nathan and Rouge had been friends since middle school. They did everything together, and even tried dating for a while. That was a mistake. There are some people who are meant to be in your life forever, and it is risky to try to make more out of those relationships than is there.

The house was small, just four rooms, but at that moment those whitewashed wooden walls looked more like home in the headlights than anywhere Nathan could imagine.

He turned the car off, got out, and went around to the trunk. As it opened, he heard the front door creek. He glanced around at the slight man silhouetted by interior lights.

"Roger Williams," Nathan stared at him.

"Nathan Kell," Rouge's angelic face broke into a smile and he ran to Nathan.

They embraced, holding each other so tight a stranger would have assumed they hadn't seen each other for years. Stepping back they held hands.

"Everything the same at Casa Kell?" Rouge asked.

Nathan rolled his eyes and grabbed two of the suitcases out of the trunk.

"That good, huh," Rouge took the remaining bags, "Well, you're home now, and we have company."

They walked to the door, and an unearthly gorgeous man whose skin glittered in the light opened it for them.

After taking a couple steps in, Nathan dropped his suitcases and grabbed the angelic beauty.

"Robin!" he exclaimed, "I didn't expect to see you."

Robin kissed him on the cheek, "Rouge told me you were going to be getting in tonight, and I thought, what the hell."

Rouge took the bags to Nathan's room.

"So," Nathan said, "Robin, are you coming to work at Wand and Weaver?"

Robin pulled away from Nathan, and sat on the couch.

Nathan sat next to him and cocked his head.

"That's not an answer." Nathan turned to Rouge who was walking past the dining table into the living room, "Why won't he answer me?"

Rouge sat down in one of the two easy chairs across from them, "We have talked about starting Wand and Weaver for a long time. Remember when you and Robin named it?"

"Junior year, we were at Tasseograph sharing a flowing tea and checking out all the hot guys we knew we could never have," Nathan answered. "And now you are changing the subject."

"Remember how special it was that Robin was there?" Rouge asked.

Nathan nodded, "Fairies rarely came into town. He was quite a spectacle. I seem to remember Lee Bushby kept coming over to the table to flirt with him," he turned to Robin, "With you. Why won't either of you answer my question."

"I eventually made Lee's dreams come true," Robin puffed his chest out. "Not right away, I had to make him beg first."

Nathan and Rouge laughed.

"I remember." Nathan said. "Robin will you help us?"

Rouge turned to Nathan, "I rented a space that will be perfect for Wand and Weaver."

"I know," Nathan leaned forward. "Why do you keep changing the subject?"

"Because I cannot help you." Robin looked off toward the empty fireplace.

"Why not?"

"Because of the growing conservatism among the Sith Thyrsa, the Fairy Queen has ordered all of Elphame to keep our distance from your kind."

Nathan plopped back in the couch, "Has the whole world gone mad? Besides, why do you care? You have never cared what Titania thought or said before."

"She won't let me work at Wand and Weaver," Robin's voice dried out, "And if I go, she will just send a warden to come get me. I have never been a fan it's true, but she has been looking for something to hang me with ever since that thing with William. This would do it."

"She can really hold a grudge, can't she." Nathan chuckled, "I'm sure the event with Alexander didn't help."

Robin shook his head, "Two lost in one century. Unforgivable."

"I'll go talk to her." Nathan made up his mind. "I'm sure I can convince her to make an exception for you. The worse thing in the world is to feel like you are alone. None of us are alone. She needs to remember that."

"Nathan?" Rouge said, "I know that look, you're not going to do something stupid are you?"

"Who me?" Nathan feigned shock.

"Yes you," Robin said. "Don't do anything that will get me in more trouble."

"Never." Nathan said, grinning like the cheshire cat.

They laughed.

Nathan almost forgot what it was like to be surrounded by friends. The three months at Thorndale Abbey were lonely.

He reminisced and laughed over several bottles of wine until the moon was high. Robin went home about midnight.

Nathan retired to his little bedroom, and pulled the covers up tight. He ran through all the things he would have to do in the morning, and before he knew it the alarm went off.

Chapter 2

Secrets and Showgirls

Nathan stumbled into the kitchen, had some coffee and a bowl of cereal. Rouge still wasn't up. He glanced at his watch. It was time to leave, but he didn't know where Rouge left the keys for Wand and Weaver.

He closed his eyes and opened his hand, "Acym me tha caega."

Two keys appeared in his palm.

Out the door and down the road, he drove as fast as he could to Fritchie Road.

The building was larger than he thought it was going to be, Two stories, with a wraparound balcony.

"Perfect," he said.

He opened the door and walked in. Half the lights were still on. The first room was a bar covered in boxes. He walked through to a large room with some tables, a large dance floor and a stage. It used to be a honky tonk or something like that. The previous owner gave away too many free drinks and paid too much for bands that no one wanted to see.

Nathan walked around. His footsteps echoed off the empty dance floor. Light filtered through the high windows in long glittering shafts.

Facing the stage, he looked at the door to his office on his right. Another door to the left of the stage led back to dressing room.

He smelled the air. The place was lived in. It smelled oaky and clean. Closing his eyes, he expected that when he opened them again he would wake up in his bed in Thorndale. He opened his eyes, and smiled.

"This is going to work!" Nathan said to himself.

He walked over to the stairs that divided the bar from the dance floor.

A knock on the door.

Nathan walked over and opened it.

A Korean man in Jackie O sunglasses, a purple sweater, and jeans squealed and rushed in to hug Nathan.

"O, girl, it has been a long time!" He posed for Nathan, "Don't recognize me do you? It's me, Shin Ki, but you know me as Harlow."

Nathan thought of the breathtaking bombshell he used to watch perform in DC. "Harlow, wow, it's hard to recognize you without the hair and hips!"

"You told us to meet you here," Harlow snatched the hand of the blue eyed boy behind him, "Remember Daniel Eisen, or should I say Marley." Harlow motions tenderly to him.

Daniel shook Nathan's hand, "You know, Ziggy's sister." He winked.

"Welcome, welcome. This is the future home of Wand and Weaver!" Nathan beamed with excitement.

"O girl, it is so big!" Harlow walked over to the dance floor.

"I am so glad you came up here," Nathan said, "I have one queen coming down from Philly. She should be here tomorrow."

"Three queens under one roof, how will we manage," Harlow giggled.

"Five in all, I am going to bring Mira Kell back and my friend Rogue will join in too. I think he performs as Rozz Painter now."

"I've seen Rozz," Daniel spoke up, "She was at Cache and Carry in Baltimore. That queen is as edgy as I am. I cannot wait to work with her."

"He'll be over later."

"I remember Rozz," Harlow said, "She did that Tina Root song, Dollhouse as a broken marionette. Powerful stuff."

"It's a Switchblade Symphony song," Nathan and Daniel said together, then smiled at each other.

"Spooky," Harlow drew out the word.

"You two were always my favorites to watch," Nathan said, "I had to beg Joseph Bhamra for your numbers. He didn't want to lose you."

"Who would?" Harlow asked, "What are we gonna be doing here?"

"Joseph told me that Marley was his choreographer, so I hoped you would do the same for me."

"Gladly!" Daniel walked over to the stage.

"And I loved to watch you Harlow, and I hoped you would be a dancer for me."

Harlow smirked and sighed "So you think I am just going to be a chorus girl? Think again. I am a headliner!"

Nathan smirked back, "That is not up to me. Marley will choreograph and give each girl her steps. Besides, we aren't going to have a marquee, so there is no top billing to fight over."

Harlow broke into a laugh, "O girl, I am just playing. I'll do anything so long as it isn't bar tending or waiting tables. This is too much beauty to hide with an apron." He gestured to his body.

Nathan laughed. "Agreed. Hopefully, I will have us a bartender by tonight, and there won't be a wait staff, at least not at first."

"What are the plans? What kind of Fetehouse will this be?" Daniel asked.

"This is a sanctuary. A place for people to go after work to forget their problems, you know, just be themselves for a change. We will hold special events for the holidays and full moons."

"Got it," Daniel nodded, "How long do we have to get ready?"

Nathan swallowed hard, "I really want to open to the public in five days."

Harlow and Daniel's mouths gaped open.

"Five days" Daniel asked, hoping he heard wrong.

"Christmas is coming, and we need to be established by then." Nathan said. "I know it is unfair to ask, but it is really important we hit the ground running."

Daniel looked like he had just been slapped. "Harlow and I have some numbers we could dust off, and I am sure the other dolls will too. That should give us a start."

Nathan hugged Daniel, "Thank you so much, I am going to leave you two here to check the place out. I have a bartender to secure. Just lock up when you leave." He pulled the keys out of his pocket and said, "Twifealde tha caega," and the keys copied.

He gave the spare set to Daniel, and headed out the door.

Nathan walked several paces away from Wand and Weaver and turned to face the tree line behind the fetehouse. He needed to find a pool of water.

He calmed his breath and listened. In the distance. . . Trickling. . . An odd warble in the stream. He walked toward the trees, making sure the sounds of water kept getting louder.

The forest was dry. The trees had tucked in for the winter and the rich scent of their composting leaves filled the air. A smokey spice also lingered on the breeze. The woods were alive with anticipation. Something was coming. He hoped it was snow. He loved the snow.

Nathan hiked through the woods for about half an hour before he spotted the creek.

The water carried a cold breeze down it. He followed its course toward the warbling sound. Someone had marked out a stone circle around a small pool of water. The creek rushed on while the pool swirled gently.

He knelt by the edge of the stone circle around the pool.

The water stilled.

Reaching toward the water, he said, "Aetyne thaere elfena aerworulde."

His reflected hand reached out of the pool and grabbed him around the wrist. Like a friend helping him out of the water, it pulled him through the frigid surface and into the world of Elphame.

Nathan knelt atop the frozen pool in the silver forest on the other side. Golden leaves coated the ground and strange birds twittered and sang songs of loss and slumber.

He looked up and greeted Robin, "You always know where I am coming through."

Robin playfully raised his eyebrows, "She is waiting for you just over the ridge."

Without another word, Nathan stood up and followed. On the other side of the ridge, a small red and white striped tent hung from the trees.

Titania, the Fairy Queen, sat on a throne made of fallen silvery branches with red velvety cushions. She glared at him, almost snarling. Her alabaster face was as full as the moon and harder than stone. She wore a flowing red gown and a gilded tiara in her red hair.

Her husband stood behind her, gazing at the ground like a defeated warrior. Another man stood to her left. He was different.

His eyes were wild like a panther, his nose was sharp like a knife, and his mouth sat on his face like a cruelly twisted twig on a snowman.

"Why are you here drymann?" Titania said like she was talking to a bad dog.

"I have come," Nathan bowed his head, "To gain permission from the Seelie Court for Robin to work for me at my fetehouse."

"For you!" The wild man snapped.

"With me," Nathan retorted.

"Why would we grant this to you?" the Fairy Queen asked. "We do not serve your kind. We are not slaves."

Nathan felt the trap within her words. "And I am master of none but myself."

The Fairy Queen licked her lips and leaned forward. "What is the advantage for us? You have nothing to offer him or me. Nothing at all."

"Your majesty," Robin bowed his head, "I want a life separate from the Seelie Court for a while. A life that is mine."

The air chilled.

"Have we not been good to you?"

"Very," Robin stood tall and squared his shoulders, "But I. . . I want to help my friend. He is our best hope among the drymann."

"And we need this hope?" The Fairy Queen raised an eyebrow, "I don't think so. His kind have always been a danger to us and our world. Now, they are even more so."

Nathan knew he had an ace in the whole, but he didn't want to play the card if he didn't have to. "Your highness, without a fierce attitude and a strong persona the world is a dangerous place. Think of the benefit you reaped when Heather escaped you. The renown and homage paid to you and your kind."

"How dare you!" The wild man lurched forward only to be stopped by Titania's hand.

"Now Jack," she said sweetly, "I am sure he meant that as a complement."

Jack? Nathan stared at the wild man to the Fairy Queen's left, *he must be Jack O'thGreen.* Nathan had heard stories of his generosity and cruelty. His moods were like the winds, at least in the stories.

Jack O'thGreen relaxed his muscles, "But Majesty, you cannot let him take Robin from us."

"I have no intention to do that." Titania turned her attention back to Nathan, "Just leave us drymann. Go and threaten someone else. Robin stays here."

Nathan sighed, "You think I am a threat? I am not a threat to you, but I could be. I know who you really are, Titania. Your real name hasn't been spoken for a very long time, and I would hate to be the one who did."

The Fairy Queen sized him up with eyes of bitter cold. Worry covered her face. "You couldn't... Wouldn't"

"I am not the kind of person who lets a mystery lie. I realized a long time ago that Titania wasn't a name. It is a title. By Albion's memory, and unless you want me to reveal your real name, you'll treat my friend better."

"See Robin," The Fairy Queen seethed, "I told you they are all dangerous."

"No, my Queen," Nathan bowed, "I am not. Ofergitole thone heahnaman Titanian, nefne heo aetegath othres." Light flashed around his forehead. "So long as you harm none, your secret is safe."

The Fairy Queen looked at him like he was a stranger. "You had a sword of Damocles to hold over me. Why would you take it away from yourself like that?"

"To prove to you that I am not the threat you think I am. I could have been, but chose not to be."

A tear rolled down Titania's face. "Robin, do you really want to go with him?"

"Yes, majesty."

"Then go," she couldn't look at either of them, "But know that we can recall you at anytime."

"Thank you majesty."

Nathan and Robin bowed and left before she changed her mind.

Back at Nathan's house, they told Rouge the story while they ate dinner. Nathan offered Robin the couch, and went to bed early. The spell caused a bad migraine and he just wanted to sleep.

Nathan and Robin pulled into the Wand and Weaver parking lot. The new sign glimmered over the door. Two other cars were in the lot. One he recognized as Daniel's, the other must belong to Castle.

They walked in, and Robin went over to the bar to set up.

Nathan greeted Daniel and Harlow.

"I've drawn up some plans for Christmas." Daniel said. "Hopefully, we can start rehearsals soon. Harlow and I have remixed a couple songs. I think you'll like it."

"I'm sure I will. Is Castle here?" Nathan asked.

"Yep," Harlow fanned his face pretending he was about to swoon, "She went back stage to put her face and tits on."

Nathan chuckled, "You think he's hot as a boy, wait till you see him in full drag. Magic."

The lights dimmed. Gold and silver spirals showered the stage with sparks. A distant shadow sashayed closer through what looked like a grove of weeping willows.

Nathan realized that Stevie Nicks' Gold Dust woman was playing.

Suddenly, a Nubian goddess stepped through the spirals. Wrapping her hands around their centers, they winked out.

The music was tuned down for her soulful voice.

She wasn't lip-syncing. Her voice was soft and sultry. Pulling the air out of the room, she waved her arms to the gentle beat of the music.

Nathan couldn't help but sway along with her.   As she sang, she pleaded with them. He fell into the well of sound.

Behind her, the stage faded into inky blackness. The light scintillated on a phantom horizon, swelling and receding with the song. Rich golds and reds lit the room like a sunrise behind the willows.

From behind her, a group of three phantom gypsies stepped out and sang along with the chorus.

She wailed like a jilted lover.

Nathan almost cried.

Gold glitter drifted from her arms as she sang and danced across the stage. She chanted the end of the song like an ancient priestess weaving a spell.

Nathan tore his eyes away from the stage and saw Daniel, Harlow, and Robin completely enthralled.

The Enchantress stopped with the music and stood in the warm faux-sunlight, "I am Lady Oban, keeper of Secrets, Revealer of Mysteries. By day, I'm Terrance Cassells, but my friends call me Castle."

They all applauded.

"I am so glad you are here!" Nathan hopped up on stage and gave Lady Oban a big hug. "This gorgeous lady helped me keep my sanity in Pennsylvania. So, Daniel what do you think?"

Daniel struggled for words, "Can you do those illusions whether you are on or off stage?"

"I can do them whenever you need them," Lady Oban beamed, "I have spent years studying the illusory arts. Haven't all of you?"

Harlow and Daniel shook their heads.

"I can do a few light effects," Harlow said, "But girl, I've never seen anything like that."

"Oh," Lady Oban brushed off the complement, "It's dead simple. I could teach you."

Harlow jumped on the spot and squealed, "Please, please, please. I know a duet, I would love to do with you, we'll talk."

"Do you always sing for yourself," Daniel asked.

"Usually. I love to sing. Occasionally, I'll do a parody or an original song."

Daniel nodded, "I can work with this."

"Good," Nathan said, "The plan is to open on the seventeenth. Adds and fliers will go out tomorrow. Everything is set." He he gestured at Robin, "This is Robin Cyd-da, he will be our bartender."

Robin waved at everyone, then motioned to Nathan, "Speaking of which, may I see you over by the bar for a moment?"

Nathan hopped off the stage and walked over to the bar with Robin.

"I don't think Lady Oban should work at Wand and Weaver." Robin said. "You can never trust a secret keeper, they are too wrapped up in their illusions."

"This from a fairy?" Nathan raised an eyebrow. "She is amazing, and will help drum up business."

"Sweetie, I am a lot older than you," he over emphasized the words. "I have known my fair share of maya worshiping secret keepers. They are always trouble. You know the kinds of things I used to do."

"Are you afraid Lady Oban will tempt you off the wagon?"

Robin groaned, "It's not that simple! Once you start playing with the fabric of reality, you are tempted to go farther, then a little farther. Before you know it, you cannot tell what is real and what isn't anymore. You become a danger to yourself and others."

"You talk about this person you just met like she's an addict."

"She is. She might not know it yet, but she is."

Nathan glanced over at Lady Oban and Daniel practicing a few steps. "You need to find a way to work together. Keep an eye on her if you want to, but don't do anything without talking to me first. We need all the help we can get. If you are right, we'll get rid of her."

"If it's not already too late."

Cyn stood outside Wand and Weaver. The drag queen checked her makeup in the windows reflection. Her sleek, golden blond wig faded to black by her scalp. Red eye shadow slashed her face around her black eyes with husky blue centers. A silver chain mail shirt fit tight on her body looping around her neck leaving her shoulders uncovered. She tugged at her short leather skirt to make sure everything was in place.

She brought to mind all of the names and faces of the people likely to be inside. Power swelled within her. Show time.

Throwing open the doors, she marched up to Nathan, "I am here for my audition."

Before he could say anything, she leapt the thirty feet to the stage and tossed a small crystal into the air.

The lights dimmed. "Crazy," a voice said as Pritam's Crazy Kiya Re started to play.

Her lipsync was tight. She danced perfectly to the music. She tossed out lines from her soul to Daniel and Harlow who joined her on stage perfectly choreographed with her.

As she sang, she twisted her hips in small, seductive circles. A coy smile framed the words. She opened her eyes wide, and looked away.

As the chorus pounded through the air, the light in the room dimmed. A solitary spotlight followed Cyn as she danced, while soft amber spots followed Daniel and Harlow.

A warm light sought out Nathan, enveloping him in an erotic warmth.

She then tossed a thread onto Nathan and fed Hrithik Roshan's parts of the song into his mind. He sang the words perfectly.

Cyn walked up to the edge of the stage, and reached out for Nathan. She beckoned from him to join her, than ran into the darkness at the back of the stage.

The light chased after her. She posed like she was shocked to be discovered, and pointed at Nathan with both hands. A second spot light focused on Nathan.

Dancing like a seductress, she stepped into the the light.

Nathan joined her mid stage, and the four danced together as if they were a seasoned troupe.

Cyn took Nathan into her arms and moved in close to kiss him. The song ended just before their lips touched.

"So boss man," Cyn's breath intoxicated him, "Do I get the job?"

"How the hell did you do that?" Daniel was fuming, "Who gave you permission to use us like that?"

Cyn shrunk innocently into herself, "I just thought it would be a good thing to show you I can sync up."

Lady Oban glared at Cyn, "Why did you leave me out?"

Cyn shrugged at Oban and flooded her words with innocence, "You just had your audition, and if it came down to a choice of you or me, I didn't wanna help your cause." Smiling at Nathan, "No hard feelings."

"I have some," Daniel huffed, "I am not your damn puppet."

"Everyone has their strings, lest we forget," Cyn blew him a kiss, "But few know how to use them to their advantage. Sorry, I upset you. I was showing off. That's what an audition's for, isn't it?"

"How did you know?" Nathan asked, "All of the others were personally invited, I didn't have an open casting call."

"I overheard you invite Oban." Cyn waved at her, "And paid drag jobs are hard to find, so I took some initiative."

"I'm pretty sure, we've never met." Lady Oban said.

"True, I am Cyn Sayshon, maybe you've heard of me?"

"I have," Harlow said, "I saw you perform once in DC. You were in a drag production of Wicked."

"That was me, I played Elphaba."

"She is really good," Harlow said, "Welcome aboard."

"Wait!" Daniel shouted, "I am not sure I can work with a puppeteer."

"I'm sorry," Cyn looked at her feet, "I just wanted to do something impressive. I didn't mean to upset everyone. Marley," she looked into Daniel's eyes, "I just wanted to work with you and other dolls so bad. Forgive me."

Daniel thought about it for a moment. "Promise you will never do that again."

"I promise. Besides, I couldn't do it again if I wanted to. Now that you know what it feels like, you'll be able to resist me. Like I said, it was a one off to show you I know how to perform."

Cyn took Nathan's hand, "So, boss, do I have the job?"

Nathan shook his head, "That was impressive, but I have all the dolls I can afford."

"I am a wizard at publicity. Hire me, and I'll make sure this place is packed. If you don't make enough to pay me, I'll leave. No hard feelings. I'm more than willing to prove my worth."

Cyn listened to Nathan's heart for a moment. He wanted to hire her, but he was concerned about the money.

"I have contacts all around here from my last tour." Cyn said, "It shouldn't be difficult for me to get the word out. I mean, what do you have to lose? At worse, you get some free publicity and a free dancer for a week. At best, you get me working for you full time."

Robin walked up to Cyn, "I love your eyes. Can you tend bar and help me clear up?

"In stilettos!"

"I vote take her on." Robin said, "Sounds like a good deal to me."

"If we're voting," Harlow said, "Cyn, your in." He did his best Heidi Klum impersonation.

Cyn smiled and gave puppy dog eyes to Daniel.

"Your look is as edgy as mine. We could do some great things together."

Lady Oban said, "I just got hired, and I don't know you so, whatever the boss lady wants."

"Well, boss lady," Cyn asked Nathan.

"We open on the seventeenth, and have rehearsals every day until then. Can you do that?"

Cyn hugged him, "Anything for you boss. I have a feeling you are going to die before you ever let me go."

Chapter 3

The Curse in the Mist

Nathan dreamed about Cyn. Horrible, terrible, delightful dreams. The kind of dreams that make you not want to get out of bed. The ones that require a shower first thing.

The shower water felt distant— the mere echo of what a warm touch should feel like.

Breakfast didn't taste right either. The flavors were hollow and old like the smell of moldy old news print. Something was wrong.

Nathan knew Robin and Rouge were talking to him. Their words barely reached his ears. He mumbled responses that sounded more like someone else talking.

He washed his face several times, desperate to wash the fog out of his eyes, but it remained. Today, they started dress rehearsals. They needed to sharpen up. He grabbed an outfit. He didn't really pay attention to which one. Then he pulled out his makeup kit.

Robin and Rouge were already at the car waiting for him. He unlocked the doors and drove toward Wand and Weaver. He overheard Robin saying something about how excited he was to see everyone in drag for the first time.

Nathan sighed, "How did everyone sleep last night?"

"Great," Rouge said.

"Well," Robin hesitated, "You kept me up most of the night. The couch is closest to your room, and well. It sounded like you had. . . A very, special guest over last night."

Nathan blushed.

"Did you bring someone home last night?" Rouge asked.

"No," Nathan said. "I just had. . ."

"Intense, active, and gratifying dreams," Robin teased him.

Nathan felt like his face was going to pop. "You could say that."

"Details, details," Robin leaned forward from the back seat to rest his head on the back of Nathan's headrest.

"There really aren't any."

"Liar!" Robin fell back, crossed his arm and pouted. "You could at least tell me who it was about."

Nathan focused on driving.

"You dreamt a little ki ki, didn't you?"

"Robin!" Nathan squirmed in his seat, "You know I would never take advantage of one of my dolls."

"I hope you're right," Robin played with his nails, "Cause if you're not, Harlow will smell it on you."

Nathan swallowed hard. He'd never felt such a strong attraction for anyone so soon. Sure, it had been a while, but this was just abnormal.

He pulled into the parking lot, rushed out of the car, took his makeup and clothes out of the trunk, and sprinted into the fetehouse. Through the dance floor to the door beside the stage, he walked in and around to the makeup counters. Castle, Daniel, and Harlow had already glued down their eyebrows.

"We start dress rehearsals today. Please take advantage of this time." Nathan looked around for Cyn, but she wasn't in yet. "This building used to be a honky tonk, so we don't know how suited to our purposes it is. We need to give the sound system and lights a good run through. And please roam around. We need to find as many wig traps and snagging nails as we can before we open."

Harlow laughed, "God save our fishnets!"

"We also need to keep in mind the spirit we are trying to bring to this place." Nathan said. "We are not female impersonators who are here to make people laugh. We are artists of illusion and fantasy, offering our patrons an escape from their daily lives. We are the embodiments of celebration, sensuality, and freedom. I believe celebration is the highest form of spirituality. As long as we keep love in our hearts, everything is a win."

Lady Oban and Robin applauded.

Harlow looked like she ate a sour lemon, "I didn't come here to dance in a temple."

"Good," Nathan sat down before a large, lighted mirror. "The shrine is downtown. This is a house of love. A sanctuary from reality."

Harlow turned to her mirror, and worked on her foundation.

Daniel's hands shook, "That is a lot of pressure."

"Not really," Nathan opened his makeup kit. "I asked all of you to come here because I knew you could do it. You already are everything we need you to be."

He watched Daniel's muscles relax through the mirror. Then started the process of transforming himself into Mira by fitting his hair under a wig cap.

Alternating between a glue stick and powder, he applied layer upon layer until his eyebrows disappeared. Next the makeup primer, followed by a generous layer of foundation, two shades.

He highlighted his cheeks, the center of his forehead down his nose and the middle of his chin. The two shades blended together to re-contour and soften his face. As he powdered over the foundation, he felt something changing within him.

Notecard pressed against his lower jaw, he applied his blush, then repeated the process on the other cheek. He blended the blush into the foundation so he looked like he had high cheek bones.

Next, she worked on her eyes with several eye shadows and liners until she had a classic cat eye. She smiled at her reflection. Mira was almost here.

After she added her luxurious eye lashes, she started to line her lips. She drew outside the line of her lips to make them look fuller. Then lipstick and gloss.

Pulling on her shirt and pants she lost herself in the lady boy looking back from the mirror. She slipped into her hip pads and bra. Then a loose, flowing, silvery knit top that looked almost like a mist, and a pair of jeans.

She pulled her wig off its dummy head, and seated it like a crown on hers. She called this wig Rebecca Romijn with curls.

Nathan was gone. Mira looked back, smiled, and winked. She was like a different person looking back.

Mira Kell looked around the room.

Daniel was now Marley Stardust, a sort of Kerli meets Tina Root Goth lolita.

Harlow looked like a 30's bombshell ready for a night out with Clark Gable.

Rouge was now Rozz Painter- imagine if Wednesday Addams decided to dress as Pink.

Lady Oban looked like Iman kitted out in this season's Alexander McQueen if that were possible. She curtsied at Nathan, "Since everyone was going edgy, I thought I would join in."

Marley walked up the couple steps from the makeup room onto Wand and Weaver's main stage, and waved at Cyn. She sat at one of the tables opposite the dance floor.

Cyn waved back, but Marley could tell it was half-hearted.

"You're late," Marley tried to sound friendly but firm, but she wasn't sure she pulled either off.

"My transformation is a private ritual," Cyn said, as she stood up. "I am here for practice, isn't that what's important?"

Marley studied Cyn for a moment. She needed to find a way to assert authority without triggering Cyn's obvious rebellious streak. "I need all the dolls to transform together to help build a sense of camaraderie. Not to mention the makeup tips and dish."

Cyn furrowed her brow, "You mean I cannot perform with the other girls unless I beat this face with them? How about I get into character early and hang out with you all while you dress?"

Was she really that private or was this a bid for power? Marley swallowed her emotions, and forced a convincing smile. "That would be fine." She realized the other dolls were watching the drama behind her. "Well, let's get started. I've seen your individual acts, and for now we'll use them as filler until we have a new stage show."

Mira took center stage, "We will perform a number every hour on the hour after eight. Audience participation is encouraged. If no one is dancing, we will keep performing until the dance floor is packed. The point is, every night is a fun night out at Wand and Weaver. I would rather not repeat numbers unless they are extremely popular or requested."

The dolls realized how much work this was going to be.

"So we will be rehearsing everyday before open," Marley said. "If any of you have any ideas for your own numbers, please feel free to let me know."

Marley lined up the dolls in the order she wanted them in, and took the queens through their steps. Sashay, sashay, twirl stage left, walk away from the audience. She felt lucky to have so many talented dancers. They took to the choreography like they had always done it.

Cyn was an amazing dancer with a intricate understanding of her body and how to move it. Lady Oban was better. Marley guessed she was trained. She mastered each move like a pro, often adding a little flourish that improved the move in a way Marley had not considered.

Mira and Rouge were both challenged. Marley could tell they were amateurs who had spent most of their time working on their makeup skills and learning how to carry themselves with little work on their performance and delivery. While they had difficulty they were committed to improving.

Harlow, well, was Harlow. A consummate performer capable of imbuing every move with a grace that distracted the untrained eye from its lack of polish and precision. With a little effort, Harlow could become a legendary performer.

Marley felt like the girls had their moves down. Harlow, Lady Oban, and Cyn were familiar with the song, Send me an Angel by Real Life, so Marley divided the lyrics amongst them, and switched to a Karaoke version. She turned up the music, dimmed the house lights, and turned on the spots and gels.

Lady Oban opened the song. Her soulful voice and sincerity added so much to the performance. The dolls knew their steps. Lady Oban sold the song and made you feel each and every word.

All three joined together on the chorus.

Harlow picked up the lyrics and played up the drama. Like a film noir star who lost her lover.

Their voices melded perfectly into the chorus.

They danced through the music. Flawless.

Cyn picked up the final repetitions of the chorus, calling out like a lost soul in desperate need of redemption. She snapped around toward the dance floor on the final lines and beams light burst from her hands. The other dolls forgot their steps, stumbling over themselves at the spectacle.

"No! No! No!" Marley turned away frustrated. Heat burned in her throat and eyes. She struggled to choke it down. She could feel the flames burning behind her eyes and could see the light on her hands. "That isn't part of the number!"

"I thought it added a little something," Cyn said cruelly.

"All it did was distract the others!" Marley forced calm thoughts into her mind. It was like trying to fit twenty people into a phone booth.

"Maybe Lady Oban could make an angel descend on stage at the end?" Cyn sounded contrite.

Why the sudden change in tone? Marley wondered. *Did she see something?*

"I can do that," Lady Oban offered.

Marley felt the fires cool and move deep down within her where they belonged. "We can try that." She looked around nervously at the queens to make sure they didn't see anything.

Cyn was stone faced and as hard to read as ever.

The last thing she needed was for her father to find out someone had seen.

Lady Oban gave her a crooked smile. She might have noticed.

Marley vowed to control herself better. Hopefully, Lady Oban was just excited to have a chance to work an illusion into the show.

"Ok, girls," Marley clapped her hands, "One more time from the top."

Nathan woke up early and dressed in a black robe, and searched through his jewelry box for a special amulet. He dreamed about Cyn again, but now was not the time to fixate on that. It was the third festival of Consualia, and he needed to get outside.

He found the amulet. It was gold with a large silver hand holding a small bronze one. He went downstairs, and found Rouge and Robin dressed similarly.

"It's just to the right of the door," Rouge said handing Nathan a broom.

Nathan always felt odd on Consualia. He was sure some wrecca had seen the ritual a long time ago and concocted the myth that witches rode around on brooms.

The three of them went outside.

Nathan stepped off the porch to the right and started sweeping. He could see the altar under the dirt and continued. Every Sith Thyrsa household buried an altar to Consus near the front door and on the three festivals of Consualia performed the rite.

It always began by sweeping off the altar. Once the stone was exposed, Nathan set the amulet on the center of it.

All three clasped their hands over their heart and recited, "In memory of the sacrifice of the giants Fritha and Scildend, and Creoda the eternal king, Modron tha Aelfena the sealer of fates, Uhtfloga the great dragon, and the first Sciman hyran, we invoke you, Consus, lord of secret counsels."

Wind rustled. The scent of baking bread filled the air.

"In your sight," they continued, "We reaffirm our promise to follow the Sith Thyrsa, the path of the giants. We swear our lives to the realm of Aernadael and her king eternal Creoda. We swear our sacred honor to the defense of Vinland, our province, and to her parliament and rightful governor, Joseph Gray. May our secrets be kept and the covenant live on!"

The breeze warmed, then cooled again.

Nathan picked up the amulet. It was almost hot. He thought for a moment about how his people around the world today awoke and performed this same rite. Well, nearly the same. Each Province named itself, and their own governor, but other than that, they spoke the same words.

He, Rouge, and Robin went in and changed into their regular clothes. He heard Rouge in the kitchen making breakfast. He entered the kitchen, and sat at the small table in the corner opposite the stove.

Tapping a small crystal ball on the counter the broadview sparkled to life. The newscaster narrated the hologram of Governor Gray, Prime Minister Tara Ward, and Lord Chancellor Matthew Weller sweeping the snow off the altar of Consus in Leifsbudir, the capitol of Vinland. Then reminded viewers to perform the rite if they hadn't already.

The images filled Nathan with a strong sense of patriotism. He voted for Ward in the last election, and thought she was doing a good job trying to fix the economy, but that wasn't it. She was the first female Prime Minister of Vinland. An accomplishment that swept her and her Unionist party to power. She and governor Gray Worked well together.

"In local news," Chloe Riley, the newscaster, looked grim, "Farmers in Seton County awoke to the horrific sight of their mutilated livestock this morning."

The image changed to an older man who had the name Jay Felton, local farmer written under his image. "I saw what did it. I heard a commotion, and when I got to the field, I saw the Dwayyo standing there covered in blood. It ran into the woods before I could hex it."

Chloe reappeared, "If true, this would be the first sighting of the Dwayyo since 1965, when the beast last rampaged through Seton and her wrecca sister county of Frederick. The beasts murders were hidden from the wrecca at the time. Two Ryukishi died containing the beast. If the Dwayyo has returned, it is only a matter of time before the attacks escalate. Stay vigilant and report any sightings to your local Constabulary or Royal Defense Office."

The smell of sausage distracted Nathan from the Broadview.

"I haven't heard about the Dwayyo since camp Green Top," he chuckled nervously.

"You were sure you saw it then," Rouge said cracking an egg into the pan.

They talked about the Dwayyo while Rouge cooked, and while they ate. Robin avoided the subject altogether.

The wolf-man pervaded their discussion on the drive into Wand and Weaver. Why was it back? How did it return? How would the authorities handle it? They didn't have any answers, but talking made them feel better, until Robin chimed in.

"Lambs were offered to the beast," he said. "That is a creepy sacrifice."

That took the fun out of the conversation and made it real somehow.

All of the queens heard the news, and were nervous.

Nathan wanted to assure them that everything would be alright, but he couldn't.

Chapter 4

The Arrow's Deep

Harlow wasn't sure why everyone was taking the rumor of the Dwayyo's return so seriously. For all he knew, it was a regular wolf or a coyote. He followed Daniel backstage and sat at the makeup counter near him. Maybe he could help comfort him, or just be close.

The door opened and Cyn walked in already in full drag.

Backstage was quiet. All the queens were lost in thought

Harlow couldn't take it. After she got her foundation on, she asked, "So, girls, when, where and why did you all start doing drag?"

Cyn spoke up, "Since the rest of you are beating your faces, I guess I'll start. My childhood was not ideal. My father and mother were never really that close. I've often thought that my mother sought out my father just to have a kid. It could have been anyone who met all the criteria on her checklist. So, as you can imagine, they didn't stay together very long. When I was ten or so, father left. Mother thought of me as her little worker bee. I felt like a slave. I used to sneak into her room and steal her best clothes. I loved the fantasy, and well, I'm damn good at it."

There was a short silence after Cyn's story.

Lady Oban went next, "I always loved fashion, and after a friend showed me The Adventures of Priscilla, Queen of the Desert, I thought to myself, if Agent Smith and Zod can do drag, I sure as hell can." She chortled and posed in the mirror, then started work on her eyes.

Mira smiled at Cyn, "Mira found me. She was an angel that would visit me in my dreams. Then one day, Rouge and I decided to dress up. I saw her in the mirror. She was a part of me. As Nathan, I was shy, and afraid of almost everything, but as Mira. . . I'm not sure how, but she was always there. She taught me how to be outgoing and how to love what nature gave me."

"Nathan answered for me," Rouge said.

"That's it? You just decided to?" Harlow asked. "Why? Because the fantasy allowed you to do and say things you wouldn't or couldn't otherwise."

"I was going through a gothic phase," Rouge said, "And I fell in love with Androgyny. From David Bowie and Lou Reed to Pete Burns, gods I thought he was hot."

Rouge and Mira broke into the chorus of You Spin Me Round (Like a Record), then laughed.

Rouge feigned like she was going to swoon, and fanned her face. "I just wanted to be like Pete, but with a touch more glamour."

Harlow looked to Marley hoping she would chime in next, but she was distracted putting on her face, and ignored the questions. "So, Madam Stardust, which number are we doing first?"

Nathan wasn't a fan of getting up early, especially when it was to do something he didn't want to do. His mother had set up an appointment at the local Sith Thyrsa Shrine for an audience with the Erythraean Sibyl.

They creeped him out. The Erythraean Sibyls were a combination of things he wasn't sure should exist apart, nor together.

The Sith Thyrsa was founded with the help of a great dragon. Dragons are such powerful creature. In fact, they possess more power than even they can use. Over time, the excess power coalesced into a pearl under the dragon's tongue. If that pearl was given to a drymann, they would change. Now-a-days, we call them Ryukishi.

Ryukishi are immortal for all intents and purposes. They are not human anymore, strictly speaking. They are the vampires of folklore. Should a Ryukishi have a child with a drymann, which they are not suppose to, but well a celibate immortal is a tall order. Their offspring is called an Erythrai after the greek goddesses of the sunset, because they are not really human either. They are usually forced into the curate, and because they often possess the gift of prophecy, they become Sibyls or Prophets.

Aimee Millar was the local Erythraean Sibyl. She was a creepy woman. Nathan had only met her a couple times, and each time he felt like there was something off about her.

So, against his will, he sat on a cold stone bench in the crypt of the shrine with his mother waiting to be summoned into see her.

He thought they were over doing it on the ambience. The room was lit only by candle light and the smell of the incense was so strong on the air he could taste it. It was unfamiliar to him. He wasn't sure what kind it was, but it set his nerves on edge.

Evelyn chanted a novena for his protection.

That bothered him almost as much as the incense.

"Evelyn and Nathan Kell," the ethereal voice called, "You may enter."

They walked through the curtain into a room of indeterminable size. The incense formed a thick fog that hung over everything like a fog in a misty rain. The room was lit by a single brazier in the center of what Nathan could see.

On the far side of the room, he could make out a vaguely feminine silhouette.

"State your question," the Sibyl sounded distant, further away than her silhouette appeared to be.

"I am afraid my son, Nathan, has not only upset the Herald but the spirits themselves," Evelyn's voice trembled.

Nathan froze. She knew. Someone told her what happened, but who? Maybe some piece of mail arrived, or a call from the abbey.

Something flashed near the Sibyl like lightening made of fire. Whispering flooded the misty fog.

"Your son will have no mortal lover." The Sibyl pronounced.

Evelyn sobbed and collapsed to her knees. "So it is true!" She exclaimed. "How can we make amends?"

The fire in the brazier dimmed. A scent of old, musty roses filled the air.

"Your son will have no mortal lover."

Nathan wrapped his arms around his mother. She convulsed with tears. "It's alright, mom. If it is true, it is probably because I will be too busy with work to settle down."

"You were kicked out of curate," she couldn't look at him, "Now, you are going to pay the price."

"Mom," her words cut him, "I'm sure that's not what this is about." He looked up at the Sibyl, "Is this because of what happened in Thorndale?"

The shadow of the Sibyl cocked its head, "You will know no mortal lover."

"That's fine with me," Nathan said, "I don't have time for it anyway. I am suppose to be at work right now."

"Nathan!" His mother chided him, "Don't you respect anything? Me, your father, your faith, anything?"

He stood up, "How dare you ask me that? I used to have to drag you to the shrine, remember? I had a disagreement with one man-"

"A herald!" Evelyn shouted, "He is more than just a man."

"I made a herald mad at me because I don't believe we are called to hate those who don't have magic!" Nathan felt like he did when he was called out before the congregation, "We are called to love and help others, not hate them! I will never believe otherwise."

Evelyn sobbed.

Nathan wanted to get her to see his side, but knew she couldn't see the difference between the institution and the faith. It would be better for both of them if he just walked out.

He felt horrible to do it, but he didn't want to say anything to his mother that would upset her more, and he knew if he stayed that would be inevitable.

With his mother's sobs stabbing his heart, he turned and walked out.

Lady Oban sat at the bar at Wand and Weaver, while Marley walked Cyn, Harlow, and Rouge through a new routine. She slid her gaze over the woodgrain. The bar was stained cherry red, darkening the grain.

Ghostly faces randomly smiled and frowned in the wood. Tricks of the eye, of Maya, that are useful to those who know how. One face in particular stood out to her. It looked like a ghost from Scooby Doo that sooner or later would have the sheet pulled off it to reveal old man Withers.

She traced a finger around it, wishing it to rise up. A soft haze rippled over it like heat on asphalt. Slowly, a copy of the spooky face melted out of the haze. It looked at Lady Oban and laughed.

"Tell me a secret," she asked.

The face rippled like a sheet in the wind. "Three secrets touched me. Three secrets touched you. Two threaten, and one saddens."

"What are they?"

The door cracked open.

Lady Oban lost her concentration and the hazy ghost shattered.

"Dammit!" She swiveled on the stool.

Nathan stood by the door, fuming.

"Hey, boss lady." She waved at him.

He nodded at her, and walked over. His footsteps were heavy, leaden. Lady Oban could almost see the burden sitting on his shoulders beating him down like a demonic, hyperactive five year old who didn't want the piggyback ride to end.

"Is everything alright?" She asked. She could have read it on him, but that would be an invasion of privacy.

"Let's see," Nathan cussed under his breath like a bawdy sailor deathly afraid of a nearby cuss jar. "I just got back from the. . . Sibyl. Not that I wanted to go. I never really cared for the practice. I mean, I believe in a lot of things, but a quasi-human who can see the future? Gimme a break. It is just another structure to maintain control over the community and keep our secrets."

Lady Oban watched Nathan twist his face and redden. She waited for the moment to speak so she wouldn't become the focus of his rage. She shook her head and exhaled sharply. "What did she say?"

"You will never know a mortal lover," he mocked an ethereal voice. "What the hell does that even mean? It wasn't even an answer to the question my mother asked."

"So, what was the question?"

"Did I upset the spirits?" Nathan's lower lip quivered "Did I upset the spirits? You will never know a mortal lover. That can't even be remotely true. It's not like I'm a virgin. I don't know why I am so upset. It's not like any of this is real."

Lady Oban shook her head, "What is real? The truth or the fact. Learn well my child, some facts are mere illusions, and some illusions are so true they have to be wrapped in a lie to take away their bite."

"What the hell does that mean?" Nathan fell onto one of the barstools. "Are you screwing with me?"

"No," Lady Oban said. "It's just something my old Conjuring Master used to say. I've talked to Rouge and Robin, and all they do is talk about you. You are one of the most faithful people I have ever met. It's possible the Sibyl meant that you will never know a love deeper than your faith. In other words, she said no."

Nathan pulled her into a hug. "I don't even care if you're right, that was brilliant." He pulled back. "You think you can tell my mother that?"

"Sure," Lady Oban beamed, "Anything to keep the boss lady happy."

Nathan cupped her hand, "May I tell you a secret?"

"If you like."

"I was afraid the Sibyl was talking about me and Cyn. I think there might be something between her and me. What, I'm not sure, but I would love to find out. If that is what she meant, then it is for the best. I mean, who has time for that anyway."

Nathan thanked her again, and went over to check on rehearsal.

Lady Oban turned back to the bar. She was glad she was able to cheer Nathan up, but she wasn't at all sure what the Sibyl meant. It was such a simple pronouncement it could be taken to mean just about anything.

It was a perfect use of Maya, like hiding a message in a kaleidoscope. The words doubled over themselves to look like anything other than what they were. Only the precise number of turns would reveal the message. Do you turn them clockwise or counterclockwise.

If the Sibyl was a fraud, she was a genius. No matter what happened, it could be interpreted as a fulfillment of the prophecy. But if she wasn't. . . Something that couldn't be put into words was coming.

Nathan's dreams were filled with Cyn again, but this time, the erotic rewards were replaced with shadowy figures pulling them apart. The words of the Sibyl echoed from the darkness.

When his alarm went off, he wanted to be excited, but that was not as easy as it should have been. Today was Wand and Weaver's Grand Opening. He wished he was nervous, nauseous, anything, but he wasn't that fortunate. He wondered if this was how roadkill felt in the moment before the strange light smashed the life out of them.

He forced himself through his morning routine, like trying to move a marionette with sticky joints and loose strings. He ate something that Rouge sat in front of him on a plate. Some of it crunched, that was probably toast, the rest was a fork of concern, then a slice of cold realization. It was really happening.

They didn't have enough time to get ready. No one was going to show up. He was sure of that. The few that did would see the drag queens, turn around and leave. How could he have ever thought this was a good idea? In a big city, maybe, but here?

He stopped himself from doubting long enough to realize he was at the door to his car. Not good. He asked Rouge to drive them in, and walked around to the passenger side.

Inertia moved him around in the seat. He focused on everything that needed to be finished before the doors opened. The time table was so unrealistic, but he hired good performers. They could handle themselves.

Robin was good at everything. Besides, he was ancient. How long did a fairy live anyway? He still looked like he was in his twenties. He always had.

The car stopped. Wand and Weaver loomed over him. He needed to get in, make sure the bar was stocked and ready. A dishwasher. . . He forgot to hire a dishwasher!

Nathan hopped out of the car and grabbed Robin by his spindly arm. "I'm so sorry. I forgot to get you a dishwasher."

Robin held back a laugh, "First, you need to remember to breathe. Second, I noticed and asked my friend, Ryan Crowe, to help out. I'm not exactly new at this."

"Well, I am!" Nathan shivered. "Thank you. So you are ready for tonight?"

"Unless someone orders Aquavit, it is still infusing behind the bar. All of the other infusions are ready, and so am I."

Nathan forced a smile and breathed slowly. He released Robin and followed him inside.

Back stage, everyone sat at their mirrors, quietly putting on their makeup.

Someone started playing RuPaul's LadyBoy over the sound system.

Everyone broke into laughter, and sang along as they worked.

"You better step up your game tonight, Rouge," Harlow said, "Or Mira might just make you lip sync for your life."

Another ripple of laughter.

Nathan made a mental note to thank Robin later. He knew he had done it.

Cyn arrived after everyone was dressed.

Mira looked at herself in the mirror. Her reflection winked at her. It was time to rally the troops.

"Ladyboys," Mira stood up and looked at them. "Tonight may be Wand and Weavers debut, but you are all seasoned professionals. That is why you are here."

"You are why we are here," Cyn said, and clapped her hands.

The other dolls joined in.

Mira blushed, "Well, thank you for that. Today is the start of something special. We have no idea how many people are going to come out tonight, so be ready for anything. The goal is to make sure everyone has a good time."

"On that note," Marley said, "I will let you know when we are starting the first number. So mill about, and get people dancing. Tonight, there is no cover, so encourage people to have a couple drinks."

"Loosen them up and knock 'em dead," Harlow added.

Mira could barely contain her pride. They were ready.

"Remember, girls, Wand and Weaver is a community Fetehouse, we need to figure out what we can do to make it as inviting and accepting as it needs to be. So be thinking of what we can do for Christmas Eve and New Years."

Rouge leaned in, "Are you going to say it, or am I?"

Mira laughed. "So let's get out there and get this party started. And girls, don't fuck it up!"

The dolls laughed and headed out.

Mira walked up to the door. It felt so far away.

Taking a deep breath, she unlocked and opened the front door. To her surprise, people were outside waiting. Some were in drag, others were dressed in their best club clothes.

They came in. Some went to the bar, others to the dance floor. A few just walked around like they were visiting a zoo. It looked like the word was out.

In a couple hours, the place was packed and the show started. *This might actually work*, Mira allowed herself a smile.

Cyn finished her number and bowed to the applause of the audience. Passion filled the air, intoxicating and sweet. The energy was perfect. She scanned the audience for Mira. She was in there somewhere. Tonight was the night.

That laugh. That hunger for attention. Cyn smiled at Mira, who was a ways off in a crowd of people she looked like she knew.

Cyn took the stairs one at a time down from the stage and worked through the dance floor. A couple times, admirers stopped her and complemented her performance or the turn out.

She kept her promise, and spread word of the grand opening far and wide. People were here from Gettysburg, Philadelphia, Baltimore, Alexandria and DC. The hotels and inns in town must be busy. Gathering a crowd was never a problem for her. It was nature, like bees to honey.

Cyn made it over to Mira who was in the gap between the bar and the dance floor. The acoustics were amazing. A sound dampener charm filled the gap so the music was soft enough to have conversation by the bar and the tables, but loud enough to feel the bass on the dance floor.

"Looks like you did it!" Cyn said to Mira with a grin.

"More like you did. These people are from everywhere!" Mira gawked at the crowd. "I don't know how you did it, but thank you."

Mira hugged Cyn before she realized what was happening.

"Let me get you a drink, we'll celebrate," Cyn held Mira's biceps.

"I don't think. . ." Mira started.

"You could possibly get drunk off one drink?" Cyn finished, "I agree. What'll you have? My guess is a Negroni. You strike me as a Campari girl."

"How did you?" Mira crinkled her face into a pleasantly surprised yet curious expression.

"I'll be right back." Cyn made her way to the bar and ordered two Negronis. When Robin handed her the drinks, she palmed him a fifty and said, "Keep the change," and winked.

She had always been curious about fairies.

Running her hands through her hair, she pretended to spruce up her do. Over her ear, she felt the needle. Pricking her finger, delighting in the pain, she infused her blood with the bitterness of despair. A quick look around. No one was looking. She dripped a few drops into Mira's glass.

Cyn picked up the drinks and returned to Mira who standing over at one of the tall tables. She handed Mira her drink, and proposed a toast, "To your future."

"To our future," Mira corrected her and clinked her glass.

They each took a swig. Cyn counted off step one in her head. She made small talk with Mira, subtly encouraging her to drink.

Mira opened up to Cyn. Her honesty took Cyn off guard. A promise was a promise though.

Little over halfway through the drink, Cyn realized Mira actually had feelings for her. *People do like a mystery.* The more Mira opened up, the more Cyn closed off. This was business. Nothing more or less. Sentiment couldn't enter the picture. Mira was a gorgeous woman, and Nathan a smoking hot guy. That was a perk. It made it all a bit easier.

It was hard to take someone she couldn't stand. It cheapened it somehow. She wondered if Mira was starting to feel the need yet.

They finished their drinks, and Cyn offered to buy Mira another.

Cyn carried the empties up to the bar. She ordered two more Negronis, and paid with another fifty. She ran her hands through her hair again, and this time infused the blood with the sweetness of love, and dripped quite a bit into Mira's drink this time. The end was easier when they were completely infatuated.

Returning to the table, she offered Mira her drink.

Mira took both of them and put them on the table. She grabbed Cyn's hand and dragged her off to the dance floor.

Cyn repeated to herself that Mira's drink was the one on the inside of the table near the center.

The bass pumped through them. How was Mira resisting the despair? She laughed and danced around Cyn.

Mira mesmerized her. Her scent was intoxicating, blinding Cyn to everything but the music. The power of the drum moved her feet. The rhythm, the dance, and the crowd melded into a seamless whole of sensuality and drive. They melded into a single being celebrating the gift of life.

Cyn couldn't take her eyes off Mira. She moved with the grace and fury of silk caught in a breeze. She was the center of the world and everyone revolved around her as if an unseen hand guided their every step. She was magic, not just a user. It emanated from her like light from a star.

Lost in the galaxy of bass and synth, Cyn fell deeper into the dance. A fire burned inside her. A burning desire that only came from deep despair, the need for another, the absolute need to never be alone again.

Had Mira somehow shared the effects of the first drink with the whole room? That was impossible. The poison was old magic. Cyn's longing ebbed and flowed like a tide, and somehow Mira was the moon pulling on her and everyone else. How?

The song ended. Cyn wasn't sure if it was the same song they started dancing to or the tenth.

They wandered back to their table.

Mira picked up the first Negroni she saw.

Cyn picked up the one near the center of the table.

"To the magic of the dance," Mira toasted.

Cyn clinked her glass.

Dry from the dance they chugged them down for the water released from the ice.

Cyn felt her throat constrict slightly. A warmth flushed her heart and cheeks. She looked at Mira, who never looked better. Perfection. No other lover could ever be as perfect as her.

That was when she realized. She drank her own poison. She wanted to cry, but how could anyone cry in the presence of such an angel. An overwhelming remorse followed for poisoning Mira's first drink. That was wrong. She would have to break her promise. No harm could come to Mira.

She asked Mira to dance.

As their skin touched, Cyn exuded the elixir of Joy onto her. The two poisons would cancel each other out. Mira would be safe.

There was no antidote to the sweetness of love. Cyn knew she couldn't save herself, but at least Mira would be safe.

Cyn felt her isolation acutely. No one could ever know.

Chapter 5

Hungry Eyes

Mira noticed something different in Cyn after the dance. She distanced herself, or at the very least appeared walled off into herself, but her eyes opened to her.

They gazed into each other. Something had definitely changed in Cyn. Her superior scowl warmed into an inviting... was that innocence?

Mira shook off the notion. That was a word that could never be applied to Cyn. What ever it was, she looked at Mira with a look that she had only heard songs about.

"I have to get back to work," Mira told Cyn, thankful her makeup covered up her blushing.

The crowd seemed to be having a good time, and Robin was busy. If this kept up, she would need to hire a barback. Maybe even some wait staff. Mira never thought she would be debating whether or not Wand and Weaver was understaffed on opening night. She knew she needed to give it some time. This could be a fluke, but if it wasn't— she grinned from ear to ear.

The night wore on, and close approached. People weren't leaving. They were going to stay until they were asked to leave. This was everything she could have wanted.

Mira jumped up on the stage, "The wolf howls in the night, hungry and longing for blood, but we are strong! Fear can only defeat us if we let it! We are fierce! We are fabulous! And the night belongs to us!"

The crowd cheered.

"We cannot allow fear to paralyze and isolate us! Together, we are strong!" Mira motioned.

Lady Oban, Rouge, Marley, Harlow, and Cyn joined her on stage. Together, they sang the Lullaby from Shock Treatment.

Everyone joined in on the last chorus. They cheered again, and dispersed.

The weekend was as busy as Friday. Mira tried to talk to Cyn about what happened while they were dancing, but she wouldn't stand still long enough for a decent conversation.

Monday came with no alarm set. Nathan wanted to sleep in and rest up from the weekend. Wand and Weaver was closed, so everyone could recharge their batteries.

Nathan hobbled into the living room earlier than he wanted to, sat in one of the easy chairs, and propped his feet up on a stool. He wanted to drift off to sleep, but his routine wouldn't allow him. He hated this feeling, like being drunk on hypnogogic wine. He wasn't awake enough to do anything, and he wasn't able to nap.

Stuck in the in between, he thanked Robin profusely when he gave him a cup of coffee. Nathan wanted to break out in song as he sipped the warm cup of waking. He laughed at himself. He knew he was out of it with that thought.

Rouge put breakfast on the table, and the three of them ate. They tried to talk, but that was nearly impossible until the coffee kicked in.

The room suddenly came into focus.

"That was one hell of a weekend," Nathan said, pushing his plate back and reclining as much as the wooden chair allowed.

"You're telling me," Robin laughed to relieve his own tension. "I was already on the Aether looking for charms and conjurations to help out behind the bar. I found several sources that recommended summoning Comus, but I'm not sure we need his influence on our patrons."

"I don't know," Rouge chortled, "That could be reasonable around Mardi Gras or Oktoberfest. Remember Oktoberfest senior year?"

Nathan rolled his eyes, "How could I ever forget? You snuck in a bottle of Fey Absinth, and talked us all into drinking some." He chuckled, "Darrell Hawker accidentally turned himself into a bird, and it took us two weeks to catch him and turn him back."

"I never was quite sure we caught the right bird, but it was good enough," Rouge giggled. "What about you?" He turned to Robin, "Ms Mira here started dancing, and just wouldn't stop. She dragged us all out to some wrecca club, and we entranced the men there."

"No," Robin shook his head in disbelief.

Nathan nodded, "O, yeah. We strolled right in off the street, flashed our fake IDs to the doorman, then proceeded to give those boys the best party they would ever have."

"In every way," Rouge gave Nathan a sly look which told the rest of the story without words.

Robin laughed so hard his face flushed strawberry red. "You little whores."

"What?" Nathan pretended to be offended, "We were just kids, well, technically."

"We were eighteen, bitch!" Rouge slapped the table.

"I said technically!" Nathan mocked a do you want to fight face. "We were free spirits then."

Robin regained some semblance of composure, "Then what the hell happened?"

Nathan, caught off guard by the question, slipped into a moment of deep thought. His eyes glassed over. He felt like his heart was made of glass and someone just hit it with a brick. The icy shards radiated out and filled his chest. "We grew up."

Robin sighed. "Take it from someone many, many, many, many years your senior, there is a big difference between maturing and forgetting how to have fun."

"I know," Nathan still felt the cold, "I just got busy."

"Don't blame me," Rouge smiled at Nathan, "My best friend moved away, and that is not something you can order from a catalog. Yet."

They laughed.

Nathan held Rouge's gaze. They had always been so close. Why hadn't he considered how moving would affect anyone else? "I think I am starting to remember how to have fun again."

"Your dance with Cyn?" Rouge asked.

Nathan blushed. "I am not sure what is going on there, but I want it to be. . . special."

Robin asked, "Have you ever felt like your life was being lived for you? I mean that is why I wanted this job. I felt like every decision was already made. All I had to do was follow the script and everything would drone on."

Rouge and Nathan nodded. They had talked about that when they were planning Wand and Weaver. They wanted to go off script.

Rouge cleared the table, and Robin switched on the Broadview for the noon news.

The Dwayyo attacked again. James Tait was attacked at his home. His pet Alce fought off the beast, and James was in the hospital recovering from this wounds.

"I don't think anyone will feel safe until the Dwayyo is gone." Robin said.

Nathan didn't want to agree, but he did. He decided to head into town for a bit to get out of the house, and to get back before dark.

Nathan drove into Schleyfield. He parked in one of the public parks downtown. The brisk air kissed his cheeks and carried the sweet smell of the bakers, restaurants, and herb shops.

More people were out than he thought there would be. He made his way to Tasseograph, his favorite tea house.

He opened the door and walked into the sensuous warmth and spice perfumed air. Concert announcements plastered the walls. Tasseograph was a '90s interpretation of beat cafe. A stool stood near a lonely microphone opposite the counter with many round wooden tables in between.

Nathan wandered up to the counter and looked over the scones, muffins, and assorted pastries in the fingerprint smudged glass case. He could hear the patrons talking about the recent Dwayyo attack.

Rachel Bird winked at Nathan from behind the counter. He remembered her from high school. She moved in the same circles as he did. It would be a lie to say they were friends, but they did hang out a lot. There needed to be a word between friend and acquaintance, chum, maybe buddy.

He knew why she winked at him. She thought it was funny to flirt with gay men. Nathan wondered if that meant she hadn't changed much. She had the skull and cross bones on her name tag. She was the manager now. Good for her.

"Long time no see," she said with odd voice of hers that always sounded over rehearsed, "I heard you were back in town. Running a bar now, I suppose you were well practiced."

All of the parties he ever threw flickered in his mind like an out of focus flip book. "Actually, Wand and Weaver is a Fetehouse. You should stop by some time. We have a killer Christmas Eve event planned."

"You think people are going to come to your club for Christmas Eve rather than spend it with their families?" She paused for a moment to let her perceived insult sink in. "What can I get you?"

"A vanilla chai latte," Nathan held his pity in check, "Well, we have booked solid for the night, so sounds like it."

Rachel pulled out a mortar and pestle in which she crushed cardamon, ginger, black pepper, and part of a cinnamon stick. She poured that into a metal tea strainer, and added black tea leaves. Snapping the top on, she popped it into a small tea pot and added hot water.

"So, what do you think about these attacks?" She asked while the tea steeped.

"I hope they will catch who or whatever is doing it soon." Nathan leaned against the counter, "You?"

"I heard the victims owed money to the Withcoren," she pronounced like it was a fact. "This is what they get for not paying up."

"Damn sheep," Nathan said, "Always borrowing more than they can pay back."

"Not the sheep," Rachel pushed his shoulder, "The farmer. We all know how rough the economy's been."

"That's not it at all," one of the patrons said.

Nathan recognized him as Louis Hussey, a local business man. Nathan knew him from services at the Shrine. His mother told him he was a business man, but not what business he was in.

"The opposition party released it because they didn't win enough seats in the recent election," Louis continued. "This is them getting a touch of untraceable revenge on the voters."

"That's a bit extreme, don't you think?" Nathan asked.

"Not when you charged the majority with not being able to maintain law and order in the provinces." Louis was sure of himself. "This proves their case, and if nothing is done about it soon, they can push for a vote of no confidence in the government and call for new elections."

His argument had a strange logic to it, but Nathan could not believe that either party would resort to terrorism to win an election. That was just too much to swallow.

He decided against arguing the point as Louis went on in detail about how everything went down. He sounded like a commentator from Mendax News.

Rachel added vanilla cream to Nathan's chai and handed it to him. He paid, and before he could leave, Greg Gladstone from Gladstone Motors spoke up.

"You're close, Louis, but you're not quite there. Neither political party has the stones to pull this off, but the Gentry do."

The Gentry was the politically correct way to refer to the Ryukishi.

"This is a publicity stunt by the Dark Gentry." Gladstone said. "They'll swoop in, save us, and gain more support for their amendments. They don't think like we do. Dragon's blood was never suppose to flow through human veins and they are the proof of it."

Before Gladstone could pull him into the conversation, Nathan thanked Rachel for the tea, and left.

He walked around downtown for a while, enjoying his chai. When it was gone, Nathan became acutely aware of the cold, and decided to go home. No one knew why the Dwayyo was back or how it would be stopped. He filed it away for later. It would be a good project for Wand and Weaver, and if they could help out, it would definitely raise their standing in the community.

Robin arrived at Wand and Weaver with Nathan and Rouge. He let them go in before him. Something strange lingered on the air. It wasn't a scent. It was more of a texture. He felt like he was standing in a room with filaments of ice hanging from the ceiling so thin they melted when touched but left no trace. He didn't know anything that would spin a web like this.

Whoever made it must have had him in mind, since neither Nathan nor Rouge acted like they felt it. Or could be it so subtle that only those born from magic were able to feel it.

He looked around, and still couldn't see anything. He couldn't sense a cause either. It bothered him. The threads caused no obvious damage, so he decided to go in and get set up for tonight.

Robin walked past the bar and through the door to the back kitchen. On the other side of the walk-in, he inspected the brownie dock. Boxes of liquor were stacked up and marked. The brownies didn't like to be seen, even by a fairy, but Robin could hear them whispering.

"Delivery counted and signed for." One of them said.

"Thank you," Robin bowed. "Could you stock these bottles for me while I prep the bar?"

A chorus of scattershot ways to say yes followed.

"Anything for the bar, set on the bar itself."

Another chorus of variant yeses.

Robin bowed again. Try as he might, he could never wrap his mind around brownies, or any kind of hob for that matter. They were various breeds of singularly focused sprites who lived to perform specific tasks. He assumed that they were once the product of conjurers, and somehow they went feral.

He reminded himself to set out an offering for them later. He couldn't do it now. They needed to finish their task first. Brownies were easily distracted.

Behind the bar, Robin started checking his bottles to make sure he had everything he needed. Scotch was where the vodka was suppose to be, and wine that was suppose to be in the racks now sat in the bourbon's spot. Nothing was in the right place.

This was not the result of a busy night and him accidentally putting a few bottles back in the wrong place. Every single one of them was in the wrong place like someone moved all his bottles around after close. He was certain when he found his angostura bitters in the wine rack.

It was probably Jack, he thought, and went about rearranging everything.

"Well, so far so good," Nathan said from somewhere behind him. "The fetehouse might work out after all."

"Of course it will. We have your vision," Robin responded, "Besides, people are scared. They need an escape."

"Yes they do," Jack's voice rang out as the door closed loudly. "The Queen has her doubts about letting you go. I mean you leave Elphame and the Dwayyo returns."

"Hey Jack," Robin didn't turn around.

"You can't think that is Robin's fault?" Nathan asked.

Jack carried a sense of dread into the room. "Actually, it would be your fault. You are the one who blackmailed our Queen after all."

Robin turned to look at Nathan, "Shouldn't you be getting dolled up?"

Nathan rocked on his heels a couple times.

Robin motioned for him to go, and he did.

"How dare you!" Robin focused on Jack. "You come in here and mess up my bar, then you say something like that to Nathan!"

Jack straightened up, as smug and superior as always. "We weren't good enough for you. You needed to get yourself mixed up with these." He motioned with his hand like he was pointing out aspects of a dirty room, "People."

"Monarchies are so 1800." Robin curled his lip like he smelled something fowl. "The queen swore to leave me alone."

"But I didn't!" Jack walked up to the bar and sat on one of the stools. "Like everything, my little pucca, you didn't really think this through. So, why don't you pack up your bags and come home."

Robin wanted to ignore him and get back to his prep, but he knew he wouldn't leave on his own. He never did.

"Don't make me banish you." Robin scowled.

Jack laughed, "Really, I thought you would make me fall in love with a mortal or give me the head of an ass. You have been around them for too long. Do you really want this to be about threats."

Robin stood silent.

"Are you going to wait for someone to die before you come home?" Jack asked.

"How do I know you didn't set the Dwayyo loose?" Robin asked. "Maybe I should ask the authorities to look into this?"

Jack returned to his cold seriousness. "You know the Dwayyo is as dangerous to us as it is to them. Why would we endanger ourselves? We are just prey for them. They hunt us down, use us up, and throw us away. I don't want that to happen to you."

"It won't. So leave."

Jack's shoulders slumped. He stood up and walked for the door. "I will save you from yourself." Then he left in a gust with the door slamming behind him.

Robin returned to his prep work. He couldn't get what Jack said out of his mind.

Cyn walked up to Wand and Weaver's bar entrance, dressed in her best Cher does Glam Goth drag. She stopped at the door. Someone was having an argument at the bar.

Recognizing Robin's voice and then Nathan's, but the third person was causing trouble. She blessed her father for his gift of preternatural hearing.

Did she hear that right? Jack blamed Nathan for bringing the Dwayyo to Seton county. Nathan wouldn't know how to summon the Dwayyo even if he wanted to.

She felt the stranger approach the door and took a couple steps back.

As he exited, she could tell he was a fairy. His willowy frame and glittery skin gave him away.

"You shouldn't talk to Nathan like that!" Cyn sneered.

"Shut up, faggot!" the fairy pushed to get past her.

Cyn grabbed him by the arm and squeezed until she saw pain in his eyes. "I don't think you heard me." She constricted her hand until he grimaced. "These children of the sun may not be to your liking, but you don't matter in the grand design, do you?"

She paused as if to give him time to answer. Twisting her thumb so her razor sharp nail punctured the fairy's shirt and skin.

"You are a child of the shadows and mists. The children of the sun, moon, and earth do not have to answer to your kind."

"And what are you suppose to be? One of them?" Pain filled the fairy's voice.

"I am a friend," Cyn easily threw him to the ground, and stood over him. "No body messes with my friends."

The fairy laughed. "If you are going to protect them from me, who is going to protect them from you?"

Shadow fell like mist from Cyn's hands. "This is not a discussion. Leave, or cease."

The fairy's eyes opened wide.

Cyn seethed with anger. The shadows thickened.

The fairy scurried off toward the tree line behind the fetehouse.

Cyn shook the shadows off her hands, and tapped out her anger.

Once she calmed, she became the model of beauty and glamor again, and marched into Wand and Weaver. She acknowledged Robin in a way she hoped meant, I've got your back.

Through the dance floor to the makeup area.

It hurt to look at Nathan, who was about a quarter Mira now. She wanted to tell him what happened, and be with him, but that was a will-o'-the-wisp. She couldn't follow where it led. It wasn't healthy for anyone.

Cyn knew her relationships always ended the same way, badly. She wouldn't survive a falling out with Mira. The poison guaranteed that.

After she was dressed, Mira approached Cyn. She reached out a hand, but Cyn pulled back.

"Did I do something wrong?" Mira asked.

Cyn couldn't look at the pain in Mira's eyes, and moved a couple steps away. "Yeah, you forgot to establish a line up for tonight's show?"

Mira froze, taken completely off guard by that. "Marley will have that to you before we open. I mean, Friday, you seemed, well, interested. And now. . ."

Cyn didn't know what to say. She couldn't lie, and she couldn't tell her the truth. "Business before pleasure, mamacita." She left for the stage.

She thought she could have handled that better, but wasn't sure exactly how. There might be something she could do. She thought about calling her father and asking him for advice.

Cyn hated talking to her father. They were too much alike, so personality conflicts were inevitable. She could imagine his reaction when she told him what happened. He would surely ask, and she couldn't lie. He would know. He would probably scold her, then lecture her. Even if he did have a solution, she wasn't sure he would share it with her.

What if he decided he needed to handle it? That would be a disaster. If Cyn could have thought of another person to ask, she would, but he was the only one she knew.

The next day, Daniel arrived at Wand and Weaver long before the others. He conceived a new number for the Christmas Eve fete. He wanted to do a lip-sync to Love Spirals Downwards' cover of Welcome Christmas.

It wasn't grinchy, more of a Christmas Star and light show, but he needed to work out all the steps before everyone arrived. Nathan was planning on dressing as Mrs Claus, so he should have the lead. Rouge would lip-sync the background.

The other queens would dance around with luminous ribbon while Lady Oban made the star move in with angels flying around it and the room.

It was a slow song, so the performance would have to be riveting to keep the audience's attention. It had to be perfect and there was no time to practice.

Daniel believed in the dolls and their abilities. They could pull it off. He put the music on and tried out the choreography, what little there was, and imagined when the angels and the star should come in, and how they should move around the room.

He lost track of time. The other queens started arriving. He joined them backstage and put his makeup on. Since Christmas was coming up, she softened her look. Velvet and bells replaced the leather and chains.

Marley gathered the queens on the stage and explained her idea for Welcome Christmas. They would perform it before the Lullaby from Shock Treatment which they had established as their closing number.

"Cyn," Lady Oban said, "I could make some angels, do you think you can control them with your puppetry?"

"I could try," Cyn shrugged.

Marley noticed that Cyn kept giving furtive glances at Mira, and was only half paying attention.

Lady Oban glamoured an angel into being.

Cyn moved her shoulder, and the angel mimicked her.

Lady Oban glamoured two more.

Cyn moved around and the three angels copied her movements perfectly. Then she glanced at Mira, and two of the angels fell on one another.

Marley wasn't sure if that was rough foreplay or if they were trying to kill each other.

"Cyn!" Marley yelled, "That is not exactly what I had in mind. I was wanting something more graceful and less disturbing."

The other dolls laughed.

"Sorry, I am a bit distracted." Cyn pulled the two angels apart with a wave of her hand.

Marley felt the anger welling up and took several deep breaths. "Lady Oban, would it be too much for you to rain glittery sparks from them like they were fireworks?"

Lady Oban obliged.

Sparks trailed from the angels as they swooped over the dance floor.

"Now the star." Marley watched the room.

A brilliant star flickered to life in the middle of the angels, swelling and shrinking to the slow rhythm of the music.

Marley restarted the song and began teaching them the choreography. It was simple. The beat was slow. Every movement and effect was meant to add to the mysterious atmosphere and warm the hearts of the audience.

She turned to watch the dolls.

An untrained eye would have thought Marley was trying to get them to perform one of the most complicated broadway numbers ever devised.

Harlow lost herself in the light show and tripped over her feet.

Cyn kept loosing control over the angels and they performed random acts of lewdness and violence.

Lady Oban stared at Marley like she was a fine piece of art.

Mira never even looked at her lyrics sheet and was obviously repeating peas and carrots, watermelon.

Rouge, well, Marley couldn't tell what was going on there. She was lost in thought or something and just stood there.

Marley sighed, hoping that would ease the fires welling up in her. It didn't. The anger rose and threatened to come out. She snapped, "Look, bitches, everyone here has a problem, or some goal in mind, or something they are running from. I get that. But dolls, why can't you just put all that shit behind you and move on? Do you want to be defined by your past forever?"

The queens froze like they had been broadsided by a truck.

Marley released enough of her anger to push the fires back down.

"Sorry about that." Marley smiled curtly. "Let's take five and try this again."

She walked off toward the bar and considered asking Robin for a shot of vodka.

Footsteps followed.

Turning around, she saw Lady Oban approaching her.

"I am so sorry, Oban," Marley said, "I just wanted to get this down before we opened tonight. I thought it was simple enough."

Lady Oban studied her carefully. "It's alright. We are all stressed out right now."

"Thank you," Marley let go of the tension in her shoulders.

"I just wanted to tell you," Lady Oban paused for a moment like she was about to deliver bad news. "I know what you are. Don't worry. I won't tell anyone. I just wanted to tell you that I know a glamour that can help."

Before Marley could respond, Lady Oban turned around and walked away.

She felt a chill rush over her like a child caught sneaking a cookie. *I might have to do something about her.*

Chapter 6

Glamour and Charm

Mira rehearsed Welcome Christmas a couple more times. She didn't feel like she had the number down yet. When Marley went to open the door, Mira snuck off to her office for a bit of quiet time. The desk was stacked with papers she needed to sort through. Some were bills, others were applications that flooded in after the success of opening night.

She didn't want to hire anyone else yet. Wand and Weaver needed to establish a bank roll before she could even consider expansion.

Behind her desk, she looked over her pin board of newspaper clippings about the Dwayyo attacks. None of them helped her make any sense of it. The attacks were random. They didn't line up with any theory she developed yet.

So far, the attacks were rare. She prayed they stayed that way.

Then there was Cyn.

Mira sat down behind her desk. Cyn was so much more and less than Mira hoped. What was going on with her? When they were together, Cyn radiated so much concern for Mira. How could she read Cyn?

How do you know if someone loves you? Mira pondered. Like so many, all she had to go on were poems, movies, and song lyrics, none of which had enough credibility to count.

Cyn's beauty, wit, and warmth filled the room every time she entered and was missed in her absence. It had to be love at first sight. What else could it be? The more Cyn pulled away, the more Mira wanted to be with her. Was that it? She just wanted to have something elusive and out of reach.

How was Mira suppose to know?

With a huff, she fumbled through the papers on her desk. She separated the applications from the bills and magazines. The muffled music beat through the wall. She needed to go out soon and help out. She just didn't want to face life right now. Everything was in such sharp relief.

A knock on the door. It was hard to differentiate from the thump of the background music.

Mira looked up and invited whoever it was in.

Cyn stepped in, closing the door behind her.

Of course it was Cyn, who else. Mira offered her the seat on the opposite side of the desk.

"Are you alright, mama?" Cyn was so cute when she was worried.

Mira shook that from her head, "Yeah, I just had a few things to look over before I joined the girls on the floor."

Cyn glanced down to papers on the desk, and scanned over them. "You have nothing to worry about."

Mira realized she could take that two ways. Either Cyn thought she was worried about the business, or she saw the way Mira looked at her.

"I just don't know how to act around you," Mira said, hoping Cyn would catch her meaning.

Cyn turned in a way that let Mira know she was blushing under her makeup. "I am just one of the girls."

Mira wanted to say, "No, you are not. I have feelings for you I just can't put into words." But instead, she said, "One of the best girls."

She forced herself not to react to that. It was one of the most awkward things she could have said.

"Thank you," Cyn puffed up in the chair, "But honestly, I think Lady Oban is a much better performer than I am."

Mira wanted to slap herself. This was the moment she could have found out if there were any potential for a relationship between her and Cyn, and instead, she allowed it to become a critique of the girls. That was her luck.

"I need to be honest with you," Mira mustered all her composure, "I think," the words caught in her throat. She couldn't push them out.

Cyn took Mira's hand, "Sweetie, this can work. You just have to believe in the vision you set up. I trust you. I believe you can do this."

Loosing the moment, Mira scolded her own cowardice and forced a smile, "I know we can. This is not about me. It is about all of us."

"On that note," Cyn said, "I have an idea for Christmas Eve. We could throw a sword in the stone night!"

Mira blinked a couple times.

"O, it's easy. We enchant and sword and thrust it into a stone. I know a charm that will lock it in until the right person comes along and pulls it out. We then crown that person the king or queen of the New Years Eve bash." Cyn obviously loved the idea.

Mira nodded, "We'll have to define the prize a bit more, but it is a great idea."

Cyn also suggested offering a blessing on the full and new moons.

Mira stood up and led Cyn out into the crowd. It was time to get to work. She could beat herself up for missing her chance later.

Oban and Daniel walked up the narrow stairway to Oban's apartment.

"Don't be so nervous," Oban said, looking over his shoulder, "I'm not the dangerous one here."

Daniel grimaced and wrinkled his nose.

Oban knew he was trying at act casual, and pretend he didn't know why he was there. As a secret keeper, he knew how hard it was to keep silent about something so personal.

He thought about when he came out to his grandmother, and when she found out he did drag. Not happy memories in the least, but he remembered that special feeling of a weight lifting off his heart.

This was the right thing to do. He wasn't outing Daniel in front of the other queens. He was doing it in private.

Twisting the key in the lock, Oban pushed open the door.

His apartment didn't look like it belonged in the building. From the cookie cutter masonry and concrete of the stairwell, they walked into a warm and inviting living room. The lights flicked on.

The walls were painted a rich burgundy with protective spirits painted in the center of each wall. The ceiling was a luxurious golden yellow with sigils and ritual designs painted in shimmering black.

Oban motioned toward a couple soft chocolate brown chairs and the couch with a coffee table between them, "Have a seat. Would you like something to drink?"

Daniel shook his head, "I don't even know why I am here." Fear narrowed his eyes. "I don't even know your real name."

"Terrance Cassells," he bowed, "But my friends call me Castle, Ms Stardust."

"Castle?" Daniel chuckled, "You have a lot of names."

Castle sat down in one of the chairs, "It's the cost of doing business. They used to call me Rook."

"Who did?" Daniel sat in the chair across from him.

"Bishop, King, Queen, and Knight, of course," Castle laughed.

Daniel's muscles relaxed, "I'm sorry I almost lost my temper this afternoon."

"I imagine you are." Castle took in a deep breath, "I know you are a Hanryu or and Erythrai."

Standing up, Daniel smirked and shook his head, "What are you talking about? That's ridiculous!"

Castle sighed. "I'm guessing you are a hanryu since you are so worried someone will uncover the truth. Not to mention that you are living free. Your dragon father or mother must be helping you hide."

Daniel stood still.

The hair on Castle's neck stood up. He was a gazelle on the savanna, and a lion was in the tall grass. He listened to Daniel's intentions: all he could hear was their two hearts beating.

Daniel balled his fists.

His knuckles blanched.

Flaring his nostrils, he looked at Castle like a wolf eyes a deer.

He stood there. Fear, anger, hate, disgust, and relief warring on his face.

Like a tree felled with an axe, he collapsed into the chair sobbing.

Castle debated whether or not to comfort him. Every fiber of his being wanted to help, but he was nothing more than a dangerous trapped animal at this moment.

"Don't worry," Castle said, "I want to help."

Daniel twisted around to sit in the chair, and wiped the tears from his eyes. "Do the others know?"

"I don't think so." Castle reached out to him.

Daniel took his hand, "Damn secret keepers," he laughed, "It's impossible to keep anything from you, isn't it?"

Castle smirked, "Part of the job." He wiggled his eyebrows and smiled. "Don't worry. I am not threatening you at all. I just want to help. I may be good at uncovering secrets, but I am even better at covering them up."

"Why? You could turn me in, collect the bounty for half-dragons, and live the rest of your life in luxury."

"Well, now that you mention it," Castle laughed, patted Daniel's hand. "I know what it is like to be hated for how I was born. It's not your fault who your parents were. Why should anyone care?"

Daniel looked away absently, "Many do."

"Then they are fools." Castle soothed him. "Like I said at the fetehouse, I know a charm and a glamour that could help you, but the charm requires your help to make, and you have to learn to work the glamour yourself."

"What will it do?" Daniel leaned it.

"It will mask your human side. To the Erythai, the Ryukishi and the Dragons, you will look and feel like a dragon. It isn't illegal to be a dragon."

"Yet," Daniel scoffed. He looked into Castle's eyes, "Will it work?"

Castle swallowed, "It'll take time. It is a complex charm to make, and the glamour won't be easy for you to learn. You are not a secret keeper, so I will have to teach you some of the fundamentals first so you will be able to do it."

"How long are we talking?"

"Months, maybe even years."

Daniel pulled his hand back and sat up in the chair. "You think I can do this?

Castle nodded.

"Then we need to get started."

Cyn thought about going into town out of drag, but then realized she would be a walking billboard for Wand and Weaver. Besides, if anyone recognized her, she could handle them.

It was early, so she focused on realism in her makeup and clothes. Few would realize she wasn't a woman. She could amp up the volume of her drag before she got to work.

She walked down the street, her high heeled boots clacking on the sidewalk. Her soft tan suede waistcoat synched tight matched her tan pencil skirt perfectly.

She entered Herbaceous Splendour with a flourish. Recognizing Toby Guest from the flyer she saw on Nathan's desk, she flashed a flirtatious smile. Old habits died hard. She had a rough idea of what she needed to pick up.

Her father, after chiding her for falling in love, told her about a potion she could brew. He said it would help some, but not to rely on it.

She hoped he was right.

"May I help you," Toby asked, approaching her.

"I hope so," she played the damsel in distress well. "I am not a potion's master."

"We do make custom brews, just tell me what you need." He pulled out a small notepad and a pencil from his apron.

He was cute. His cherubic face wore a slight coat of dirt and his hands looked like they had tended plants all morning. Though she could tell he was much older, he looked like a teenager. He couldn't have been more than twenty.

Cyn blushed as she focused her thoughts back on her task. "O, thank you, but I want to learn. I need a mortar and pestle, and a cauldron."

Toby pulled the items off their shelves, as well as some charcoal.

Cyn thought for a moment whether she really wanted to do this. She never covered up who and what she was. Part of her felt like she would betray herself if she went through with this. In her heart, she wanted to be with Nathan, and this was her only option.

"Are you alright?" Toby asked.

"Yes," Cyn pulled herself back together. "Why?"

Toby chewed on his bottom lip a little, "You seem to have something other than potions on your mind. Are you planning on making a love potion? Because if you are, they almost never work."

Love potions are simple, honey. Cyn thought. "O, no. I just have a lot on my mind. I work at Wand and Weaver, that new fetehouse out on Fritchie Road."

"I've heard good things."

"Maybe you should come out sometime?"

Toby blushed and looked away. "What else can I get you?"

Cyn basked in his embarrassment. She loved to make cute boys squirm. It was like candy. "I need some Willow bark, sap from the Austras Koks, root and flower of Molu, and three pieces of laguar."

"Laguar?" Toby started, and looked up from the list he was writing. "True water ore is expensive. Most potions can be made with tap or spring water."

"The recipe calls for laguar." Cyn watched him write it down.

"If you don't mind me asking, what are you making?" Toby scanned the ingredients list. "I don't know of a potion like this. Since it has Molu in it, I presume it is protection potion of some sort. Is it to ward off the Dwayyo?"

Cyn stood silently.

"Cause if it is," Toby continued, "I might want to make some to sell here. I've gotten a lot of requests for such a potion."

"It is not for the Dwayyo." Cyn hoped that would suffice. "Do you have everything I need?"

Toby looked over the list again, "I have everything but the laguar. I don't usually keep any ar in stock. It's too expensive, and there isn't much demand. It doesn't last long on the shelf either. How soon do you need this?"

"As soon as you can get it." Cyn gave him a smile that promised great rewards.

"I'll call my supplier." Toby took the list and walked through a curtain into the back room.

Cyn huffed. She'd wanted to make a potion before work. *Should I go into Baltimore or DC? I bet I could find some there.* She decided against it. She didn't want to drive all around the state looking for laguar.

More than likely, it was a specialty item everywhere. Pure elements tended to evaporate quickly.

She wondered what was taking him. She didn't order any controlled substances. He was probably checking the aether to find out what those ingredients could make. What if he figured it out? She would have to handle him.

Toby emerged from the back room, "The soonest I can have you some laguar is the 26th. Is that alright?"

Cyn sighed. "I will pick up everything then."

Nathan sat in his office and looked out the window at the empty parking lot. He glanced at the bills, invoices, and orders on his desk, and then back out the window.

Everything with Wand and Weaver was going well, almost too well. He didn't really trust it. Tomorrow was their first big event, Sword in the Stone night. If that went well, he would be able to relax some.

He knew it was a risk for him to hang so much on a Christmas Eve party, but that is the type of event that a fetehouse should excel at.

Someone tapped lightly on the door.

Nathan shook himself free from his thoughts. "Enter."

The door cracked open.

Marley peeked her head in. "If you're busy, I can come back."

"I know I need to beat my face," Nathan waved her in.

Marley walked in and closed the door.

Something wasn't right. Marley was dressed and painted, but wasn't in character yet.

"What is it, sweetie?" Nathan asked.

"I think I am the reason the Dwayyo is here." Daniel muttered through Marley's lips.

Nathan straightened in his chair, and waved for Marley to sit.

Marley shook her head; her earrings making a muffled clacking under her hair. "I don't think you heard me. I am the reason the Dwayyo is here."

Nathan sighed, and watched her shoulders slump.

"I heard you," he said, "I just can't figure out why you would say, much less think, anything like that."

"My father," Marley bit her lips and inhaled sharply, "My father told me that darkness and death would follow me if I left the family... business."

"Why would he say something like that?" Nathan ran down several possibilities in his head, "Are they Mafia or something?"

"Or something," Marley held her own wrist in front of her, and looked down like a child in the principal's office.

"What does that mean?" Nathan rolled his chair back a couple inches, "What are you talking about? You can trust me. Does someone have a contract out on you?"

"No," Marley didn't change her pose. "It's nothing like that. He just told me..."

"That death and darkness would follow you." Nathan shook his head, "What could possibly make you believe that?"

"Wouldn't you consider a giant wolf monster as death and darkness?"

Nathan couldn't believe what he was hearing. He wanted to punch Marley's father in the gut. "If anyone in this room brought the Dwayyo upon us, it was me. I, personally, offended a Herald. I was kicked out of the novitiate, and I am the one who was unapologetic about it. I may have even performed an act of sedition against the Fairy Queen in Elphame. I think that trumps anything you could have done."

Marley shook her head slowly, but didn't say anything. She just stood there for a while shaking her head like she wanted to say something.

"Are you alright?" Nathan asked.

Marley looked up and nodded. A single tear ran from the corner of her eye.

"Don't worry, hon." Nathan stood up and put his arm around her, "We'll get through this. Now, I have to go make sure everything is ready for tomorrow night."

Chapter 7

Sword in the Stone

Mira posed before the full length mirror backstage. This is what all the work was for. She was dressed like Mrs. Claus if she were a star from the golden age of Hollywood. Candy red velvet and snow white fur trim, her hood crowning her crystalline hair. Tonight was their first fete. The future of Wand and Weaver rested on pulling this off.

Cyn dressed like a snow maiden from japanese folklore, and Harlow looked like she should dancing with Danny Kay in White Christmas.

Mira stepped out onto the dance floor. She could hear Rouge upstairs getting ready for the kids. Holly and tinsel trimmed every line. The lights drew snowflakes and stars in random patterns around the room.

The bar looked like a place the ghost of christmas past would bring Scrooge to remind him of better days.

Out the door onto the porch, Gingerbread choruses sang A Winter Wassail. Garlands with fairy lights draped from everything. Robin charmed the air so it looked like it was snowing. The first reservations arrived.

Marley, who dressed as a Christmas Elf, joined Mira on the porch. Together, they greeted the families as they arrived. Marley ushered the children upstairs to the winter wonderland, and Mira offered the hospitality of Wand and Weaver to their parents.

No one canceled their reservation, and they kept coming. Mira was glad she placed a full order for cakes and pies from Two of Tarts. She doubted there would be any left overs.

She kept expecting to see her sister. She said she would try to bring the family out. But when the last family arrived, she knew they weren't coming. It stung a bit, but Mira was determined not to allow anything to cast a shadow over tonight.

Mira stepped into the packed house.

The sword in the stone sat just off the dance floor. A long line of people waited for their turn to give it a tug and see if they were the one. Mira didn't know what the trigger was Cyn set up.

Some people pulled on it with all of their might. Others hurled enchantments at it first, hoping to loosen it. So far no one had made it budge at all.

Harlow loved the outfit she picked out. It was classic Christmas, and just different enough from Mira's she didn't look like she copied it. The red was darker and richer for a start more of a crimson than scarlet, with a double slit to free her legs for dancing. Just white fur lined her shoulders, no sleeves.

The color matched her golden skin perfectly. She matched it with a blond wig that gracefully parted in the front to reveal her right eye and part of her left and barely reached her shoulders.

She blew herself a kiss in the mirror, and gathered her resolve. Today was the day she would reveal her love to Marley. She had practiced a number with Lady Oban, and knew Marley would devote her attention to the stage when she heard a song she hadn't chosen.

Harlow heard the music bound to life, and the voices of the patrons coming in.

Leaving the backstage area, she bopped her way across the dance floor. A few people danced with her, then more, then even more. Soon, the fetehouse took on a life of its own.

She twirled her way over to the bar, and winked at Robin, who was busy making drinks.

She climbed up the stairs. The illusory snow started falling about half way up. She could hear children laughing. Atop the stairs, she looked around for Marley.

Lady Oban and Robin glamoured every corner of the loft. She knew what the unfinished loft looked like, and couldn't recognize a bit of it.

A starry night sky stretched out as far as the eye could see lit by the full moon and drifting fairy lights. Snow covered what honestly felt like grassy ground. Two snow forts opposed each other over where the Stage and dance floor were. A hill sloped down from behind one of the ice forts for kids to sled down.

Harlow considered taking a run on it herself. Marley came up the stairs with some kids. They ran for the ice forts and started a snowball fight.

"They did a good job, didn't they." Marley said rather than ask.

Harlow watched the pixies around the fire pit over the bar spring to life, hooting and catcalling.

More kids arrived. Some went sledding, others joined the snow ball fight, and the rest ran to the fire pit to play with the pixies.

If she didn't know better and it had snowed earlier, she would have sworn she was outside.

Marley was so close. Harlow just wanted to blurt it out, but she didn't want to get the wrong response. That is why she concocted the plan with Lady Oban. Always test the water before you jump in, so you don't end up cold and screaming.

It was almost time.

Harlow turned to Marley, "We should probably head down stairs and see if they need any help."

Marley nodded, "I can't be away long."

As they walked down the steps, Harlow rubbed a finger across one of the rhinestones in her left earring, which sent a message to Lady Oban to get to the stage.

Wand and Weaver was packed. The line to the Sword in the Stone was still long, no one had pulled it free yet.

Harlow and Marley mingled through the crowd toward the dance floor.

The music stopped. Everyone looked around.

The fast kick drum burst from the speakers.

Harlow clicked her heels together. Silver light flashed from them. She and Lady Oban speed up a version of Kiss' Who wants to be Lonely.

The guitar came in.

Harlow took a step up, and the light from the shoes created a platform under her. She climbed into the air like she had stairs.

She sang for herself. Looking right into Marley's eyes, she sang the first line, then broadened her performance to include everyone.

She walked over their heads as she sang, bopping along to the beat of the music.

Harlow hopped onto the stage by the first chorus, and Lady Oban joined her as a background singer.

In light of the Holiday and the Dwayyo attacks, the song took on a significance that it ordinarily wouldn't have. The crowd really got into it.

Harlow watched them clap to the beat and sing along with the oos and ohs in the song.

When the guitar solo started Harlow looked over to Marley. She and Rouge were dancing with the guests.

The last couple repetitions of the chorus changed slightly. Harlow realized that while no one wants to be lonely, tonight, she would be.

The song ended, and Harlow watched Marley applaud with everyone else.

Harlow bowed. The performance was a hit, but it missed its mark. She needed to draw up the courage to just say something. The applause felt hollow. The room was a little colder.

Mira applauded with everyone else. She even let herself whistle a couple times. Before the crowd quieted, the music was back on, and the dance claimed them again.

Marley looked up like she forgot something and rushed for the stairs.

No one had pulled the sword from the stone yet, and that worried Mira. What if no one met the criteria Cyn set? She thought about asking her what they were, but decided to give it a little while. The longer the Sword stayed in place, the more shooters they could sell to people in line.

She made her way over to the bar. Robin looked like he was a Hindu god of mixology. He moved so fast. Pour, pour, pour, cap, shake, pour, serve, on to the next drink.

Mira looked around for a place she could be helpful.

The crowd roared.

Light glinted over their heads. Someone pulled the sword from the stone.

Mira made her way over. Golden light shown from the stone, illuminated a beautiful arabic woman with shoulder length black hair, jeans, and lovely purple shirt.

Raising her hand in triumph, Mira leaned down and asked her name.

Marley turned on Rupaul's Champion.

Mira lead her through the crowd to the stage with the sword high above their heads.

Once they stood in center stage, Marley turned down the music.

"Grace Ahmad has pulled the Sword from the Stone!" Mira announced.

The crowd roared again.

Lady Oban joined them on the stage carrying a royal blue velvet pillow on which rested a silver and crystal crown that looked like it was made of ice.

"Kneel please," Mira whispered in Grace's ear.

She blushed and gave in to nervous laughter, but knelt.

Mira stood behind her and lifted the crown off the pillow. Holding the crown over Grace's head, "It is my honor to crown you, Grace Ahmad, the Queen of Wintertide." She rested the crown on Grace and made sure it was on secure.

Grace still chuckled a little, but blushed more.

"As our Queen of Wintertide," Mira helped Grace to her feet, "You will preside over the new years celebration. Which means that you and five of your friends will join us as our guest. The new year is coming and will bring light, love, and harmony to Seton county!"

The audience applauded.

Mira, noticing the time, signaled for the others to join her up on the stage.

They performed Welcome Christmas. The guests sang along with them. When they were done, they bowed to the thunderous applause.

"Merry Christmas, everyone! Now, get to bed so St Nick can visit. See you all real soon."

The guests clapped again. They settled their tabs and filed out.

Mira looked around at the divine mess.

Everyone started cleaning up.

"We can do that later," Mira said, "Stop cleaning, its time to get home!"

"Before you go back to change," Cyn said, "Santa Kell bought you all presents. They are at your stations. She was too shy to take credit, and I want to make sure she got what she was due."

Mira didn't know what Cyn was talking about. She didn't have the money to do anything like that.

She went backstage and a beautifully wrapped gift sat in everyone's station.

The queens opened them. Everyone pulled out a white gold necklace with an endless knot pendant inscribed, "Wand and Weaver, 2010" in beautiful calligraphy from Kessho-sui. They must have cost a fortune. They were all the same.

Mira opened hers. It was a triquetra interlaced around a circle.

Nathan woke up bright and early on Christmas morning, a habit he picked up when he was a kid. He rushed to get dressed and beat Rouge to the Kitchen. He whipped up a batch of blueberry and banana nut muffins, and laid out the stockings he had prepared for Rouge and Robin, who was now sleeping in a Rouge's room.

Rouge always wanted a bunk bed, and Robin gave him an excuse to get one.

By the time Rouge and Robin wobbled into the living room, the muffins were laid out on the table around the small tree. They exchanged gifts while they had breakfast. None of them really had a lot of money.

Nathan got the two Erin Morley novels he wanted. Nathan and Rouge pooled their money to get Robin a Home Sweet Home Charm. Rouge got the new A Chained Thirst album and concert video.

After breakfast, they got dressed, and headed out.

Nathan dropped Rouge off at his parent's house, then drove to his own. Robin wasn't going back to Elphame, so he joined Nathan.

Dinner at the Kells went as expected. They opened presents, ate a feast, after which Nathan's father and brother, Ian, disappeared to tinker with something. His sisters got into an argument, and his mother looked sad and disappointed.

He picked Rouge up on the way home. Rouge had a wonderful time and regaled them all with the legend on the way.

When they got home, Nathan went into his room. He wanted to give himself a gift. He lit some candles, and invoked his guardian.

Once he felt her close to him, he asked her to show him a glimpse of his future. Would he end up with Cyn.

His vision dimmed. He felt his guardian pull closer.

He was somewhere else. The room was lit by fire, candles maybe torches. It was too hard to tell.

The walls were made of stone. There wasn't enough light to tell if they were cave walls or masonry.

He held someone's hand. He looked to his right. Cyn was with him.

"Are you sure you want to do this?" She asked.

Nathan felt himself nod, and step forward. "It is the only way." He swallowed hard. "I am here! I have considered the price and I accept!"

Something moved in the shadows. It was heavy. A dragon stepped into the light and belched fire at them.

The wall of heat hit them and Cyn projected some kind of a shield in front of them, holding the flames at bay. They were together.

Heat boiled Nathan's skin.

Cyn faltered.

The flames rushed at them.

Blinding pain.

Burning.

Nathan jerked back to the present.

"This is what must be," his guardian said.

Nathan sat there stunned.

"The Sibyl was right." He blew out the candle.

Chapter 8

Blood at the Doorstep

Nathan ambled to his car. He needed to get out and get away, after spending the last couple days in his room pretending to read his Erin Morley books. He couldn't get the image and worse the sensation of being roasted alive by a dragon out of his head. He'd heard that Ryukishi could take on a draconic form. Suddenly, he shared Marley's concern about them coming to deal with the Dwayyo.

He sat behind the wheel for a while before he started the engine, mind racing. There had to be a way to change the future.

Fate was an intricate thing. As the threads of the present weave together, the future becomes increasingly fixed. When the founders of the Sith Thyrsa saw the destruction of the magical community during the approaching inquisitions and crusades, they cut the threads by pulling magic out of the world. They added a new thread to the tapestry and removed an old one, changing the design in the process.

Nathan thought about ways to change the present. Nothing immediately came to mind. He started driving. At first, he had no destination in mind. He was a planner, and wondered if he allowed more room for chance, then maybe he could avoid the flames.

Approaching Schleyfield, his thirst asserted itself. He didn't want a drink, his tongue felt like it was missing a flavor- Vanilla Chai.

His mouth wasn't dry. He just needed to go to Tasseograph and get a drink.

He didn't have such a pronounced craving often, so he decided to follow it. Finding a parking spot was easy. Most people were at work.

The crisp December air carried all the spice and richness of the downtown shops to him like a gift. They soothed him, along with the gentle burbling Cane Creek nearby.

Nathan walked over to the stone retaining walls snaking along side the creek through town. He listened carefully and could hear the Naiads singing in the water.

Following the creek to the road Tasseograph was on, he walked over the concrete bridge. He said a quiet goodbye to the Naiads, and continued.

He reached Tasseograph, and greeted Rachel as he entered. Part of him thought that by now he should be able to ask for his usual, but he didn't want to embarrass her if she didn't remember. He ordered a vanilla chai.

"Of course," Rachel smiled at him, "I have some Hesaret cream in if you would like it instead of regular cream. It is suppose to bring good luck, and it has a richer taste. It pairs better with the vanilla."

"I could use as much luck as I can get," Nathan said, "I'll try it."

While Rachel made his chai, Nathan glanced around the room. His gaze snagged on a diamond.

At a table by the window, a handsome man read a copy of The Portrait of Dorian Gray. His face was soft but manly. Perfect blue eyes floated under his black brows. His high cheeks smiled as he sipped his tea. Nathan took in his midnight black hair, cut short, but not too short. Everything was perfect.

He wore a blood red v-neck sweater that complemented his creamy skin. Nothing was out of place.

Nathan looked away and back again, sure he was a fantasy, or that he missed something. He was a feast for the eyes in every possible way.

Rachel handed Nathan his chai in a capped paper cup.

Nathan blushed, it took about ten minutes for Rachel to make a tea. She was a perfectionist, and all her work paid off. But that meant he was staring at that stranger for ten minutes. Possibly, drooling.

He nervously touched around his mouth to make sure he hadn't.

Sipping the chai, he lost himself in the rich creaminess of it. The Hesaret milk made it more like a meal than a beverage.

"You were right," he said, ripping his attention from the stranger. "This is a lot better."

Rachel blushed in that under confident way she had.

"You should come out to Wand and Weaver this week," he said, hopefully loud enough for the stranger to hear, "There is no cover change until the new year, and I would gladly comp your drinks to thank you for this."

Rachel reddened more, and mumbled something softly, and rushed off to check the ovens.

Nathan returned his attention to the eye candy by the window. He wanted to talk to the gorgeous stranger, but couldn't persuade his feet to move. His confidence flushed out of him.

The stranger stood up, and acknowledged Nathan with his perfect blue eyes. He tossed his cup away in the trash and left.

Nathan lost himself in a fantasy as he watched the stranger walk away. He wasn't sure how much time passed while he was lost in fantasy, but he snapped out of it when Rouge entered.

"There you are," Rouge said, "You have been acting odd since Monday, what's the matter?"

Nathan bought him a tea, and told him about everything.

It circled the streets, looking down. It watched for Nathan. Following him from shop to shop, beating its wings and wishing for thermals to glide on that the cold air would not allow for.

It watched Nathan leave a candle shop alone, and walk back toward his car. The dark night sky provided the best camouflage no one could see it from up here. It could watch without fear.

The mission was clear, and so was the target.

Nathan entered his car and started driving.

The night bird flapped its wings and easily followed over the winding roads. Its vision was acute, able to see Nathan's car through the tangled branches as he drove into the country toward his home. Thankfully, it was winter and the foliage didn't add cover.   A strange taste on the air. Musky and thick, reeking of gore.

The small Regen pulled up to the little house in the middle of nowhere.

The night bird flew lower.

Nathan's house was in a clearing in the woods. A large maple tree stood in the front yard, not far from the door. It was encircled by forest.

Desire. The night bird felt a hunger from the tree line to the west of the house, and listened intently.

Heavy breaths.

Nathan opened the door, and slipped out of his car.

The thing in the tree line moved.

The Dwayyo stepped into the clearing and howled.

The night bird could smell the fear rolling off Nathan.

The beast stood at least nine feet tall, and looked like a crossbreed between a gray wolf and a Sasquatch. It growled and snarled.

The night bird began a dive.

Nathan froze in the presence of the monster.

The Dwayyo bounded toward him, taking huge strides. Its claws and teeth glinted in the sparse light like blades.

The night bird screeched like an owl and pulled its bat-like wings in close to its body. It shot down from the sky like a bullet. Pouncing onto the Dwayyo, it drove the talons on its feet and wings through the beast's thick fur into its rock hard skin.

The Dwayyo stumbled back. It hadn't expected the night bird's slashing attack.

It grabbed the winged thing by its human-like shoulders and tried to push it back.

The night bird leaned into the attack revealing its monstrous maul of gnashing teeth.

The Dwayyo punched at the unnatural chimera, dislodging it and knocking it to the ground.

It landed on its heel talons and stood about six feet in height. It screeched at the towering bulk of the Dwayyo.

Lunging forward, the Dwayyo threw its weight behind its massive jaws.

The chimera leapt into the air, and watched the wolf-man slide harmlessly under it. It twisted, and sunk its claws deep into the Dwayyo's back ripping fur and fresh flesh.

Black blood spurted from the wounds.

The Dwayyo howled in pain, and reached back for the night bird, just missing it as it took flight again.

The bird watched Nathan run into the house.

The Dwayyo sneered at the sound of the slamming door.

The night bird screeched and dove at the other beast's head, hoping to take out an eye.

The dwayyo ducked and slashed at the chimera.

Feeling the beasts claws drag impotently across its side, the night bird cackled.

Enraged, the Dwayyo howled and ran for the forest.

The night bird considered chasing it, but knew it didn't have enough strength to kill it, and it didn't want to leave Nathan defenseless should the beast double back.

With a victorious cry, the night bird flapped its mammoth wings and rose high above the clearing and the little house. It circled, mindful of even the slightest movement on the ground until the sun broke into the night sky.

Chapter 9

Magic Man

Nathan was still shaken when he arrived at Wand and Weaver from the events of the night before. He didn't sleep well. The Dwayyo came for him, and if it wasn't for that strange beast that fought it off, it would have had him. He had to go to work, but he was concerned about going home. He thought about moving his, Robin's, and Rouges things into the loft while it wasn't in use, but the fetehouse didn't have any facilities to bathe or shower. That would be a problem.

He invoked every protection charm he knew before he left.

Robin spent the morning building fairy rings to draw pixies into the yard. They wouldn't be able to protect them, but they would be a good early warning sign the beast was near. The pixies would seek shelter in the house at the first sign of trouble. What they did after that was a problem.

Rouge enchanted every wall, window, and door to make them impenetrable to any unwelcome visitor. This incantation was the source of the legend that a vampire couldn't enter a home without first being invited. Of course, there was no such thing as a vampire, unless you counted the Ryukishi.

Nathan, Rouge, and Robin rushed from the car into Wand and Weaver.

Nathan's hands shook. He focused his mind and rested in the comforting arms of his guardian for a moment. That should have returned peace to his mind, but the best his guardian could do was inspire his actions. She couldn't manifest and fight off the beast if it attacked again.

Walking backstage, he smiled at Cyn, Harlow, Marley, and Lady Oban. Cyn was already in glamazon drag, and looked like she was ready for war.

Cyn smiled at Nathan, and looked hurt when the smile wasn't returned. Why did that bother her so much? There was nothing going on between them as far as Nathan could tell. Cyn flirted with everyone. Nathan was no different from anyone else.

Nathan sat at his makeup mirror. Trembling, he tried to put his makeup on.

"Are you alright, sweetie?" Cyn asked.

Nathan closed his eyes. Pain covered his face like a mask. "The dwayyo tried to kill me last night." He heard the room gasp. "It charged out of the woods and would have killed me if," he tried to think of a way to describe that strange winged creature. "This bat winged thing fought it off. Rouge thinks it was a snallygaster. I am not sure there is such a thing. Whatever it was, it saved my life."

The room was silent.

Opening his eyes, he glanced around at their astonished faces.

"You must have a guardian angel," Cyn said.

Marley nodded, "Someone is looking out for you."

"Could you make out the form of the creature?" Lady Oban asked.

"It was dark, and I was so," Nathan almost said frightened, but that word was utterly inadequate for the job. "It had bat-like wings, talons on its wings and feet, a mouth full of razor sharp teeth, and," he considered the moonlit creature for a moment. "It looked almost like a person. I don't know what it was."

"Maybe you aren't meant to," Lady Oban said, returning her attention to the mirror. "Just give thanks and be happy you're alive."

Nathan tried to start his makeup again, but his hands shook too much.

"Let me, baby," Cyn put her hand on his shoulder and spun him around in the chair. "Today, you will have visage a la Cyn."

Nathan warmed. It felt good to be taken care of, especially when everything was going crazy around him.

"We all have our duties and obligations," Cyn said as she applied Mira's face. "Some need to be fulfilled, while others need to be cast aside. You are the mother of our little community. You can share your fears and doubts with us. We'll help you carry them. But out there, you are Mira Kell, the beacon of hope and faith. The light of Wand and Weaver."

Nathan shrunk away from Cyn. He wasn't used to being flattered like that.

Cyn made him look at her so she could continue her work. "You may not feel it today, but it is who you are. We all believe in you. That should be enough for you until you believe in yourself."

Nathan smiled.

He felt the transition into Mira taking root in him. Mira was fierce, the embodiment of everything Nathan wanted to be. She was more than a character he pretended to be. She was always with him.

Makeup on, posture tall and proud, Mira donned her wig and got dressed.

Mira looked at Cyn. She was grateful for the help, but still couldn't discern a motive. Was Mira Cyn's employer who needed to be strong for business, her friend she didn't want to see frightened, or someone she cared about? Whatever the answer, Mira knew she wanted to find love, life is too short to live without it.

Turnout was great that night. Wand and Weaver had grown in popularity. People came from all over for the music and entertainment. Mira was so proud. Marley and Lady Oban performed on the stage.

Mira greeted the guests, and danced with a few. She looked over to the door as it opened.

A man dressed all in black entered. Mira recognized his perfect blue eyes, high cheeked smile, and midnight black hair, cut short, but not too short. It was the man from Tasseograph.

Harlow grabbed onto Mira's arm like she was about to fall, "O, girl, did you see the glory that crossed our threshold?"

Mira chuckled, "Yeah, I saw him the other day." She wondered if he heard her drop the name of the fetehouse when he invited Rachel, or if he just found Wand and Weaver on his own.

Harlow pursed her lips and raised an eyebrow at Mira, "Did you? You tramp, go say hello to him." She pushed Mira at him.

Mira looked around, Rouge was busy serving drinks to the tables, and Harlow was too busy staring at the gorgeous man in black. Everything looked like it was well in hand. She could take a moment for herself.

Walking over to him, Mira rehearsed in her mind what she would say when she arrived. She felt like she had never greeted a stranger at Wand and Weaver before.

The man in black stood in line for the bar. That was it.

"I am Mira Kell," she offered her hand to him, "Mistress of this establishment."

He kissed the back of her hand rather than shake it. "I am Emrys," His voice was as perfect as the rest of him. That sweet masculine voice able to make ice melt and lovers to throng about him.

"Glad to meet you, Emrys," Mira forced herself not to swoon. "May I get you a drink?"

"I would love a Rye Manhattan, two cherries, please."

It was a perfect drink. Strong, classic, improved by the addition of the Rye Whiskey to the sweet vermouth. Two cherries. He either like maraschino cherries, or he was flirting. Mira cursed her inexperience.

Robin was busy, so Mira made two Rye Manhattans. One for herself and the other for Emrys. That was a good name. She wondered if anything about him wasn't perfect.

She returned with the Manhattans and waited for him to take a sip.

"You did a good job on this." He smiled. "This isn't my usual scene, but those two on stage are good."

"That's Marley Stardust and Lady Oban," Mira beamed with pride, "They are two of our best performers."

Emrys took a swig of his Manhattan, and blushed. "It is a little loud in here, can we go outside for a moment."

Mira could hear him clearly, but didn't want to argue. She flagged down Harlow and asked her to cover the floor for a moment.

Emrys led Mira outside and blushed again, "I have an ulterior motive for coming here tonight. I saw you at Tasseograph yesterday, at least I hope it was you. O, Feoras, I hope it was you, or I am making a complete ass of myself."

"It was me," Mira said.

"Good," he swallowed, "Great. I listened in to your conversation with Rachel." He closed his eyes and braced himself like he expected to be slapped. When nothing happened, "I heard you worked here, and I knew I just had to meet you."

Mira wanted to break out into a song and dance celebrating those golden words like they did in the movies, but held it all inside. "I'm glad," she said once she could make words, "I wanted to talk to you too, but couldn't find the nerve to do it."

"So," Emrys looked like a lost puppy. "Hello there." He waved.

Mira couldn't help but laugh.

"I'm not very good at this," he said, "If you can't tell."

"Neither am I."

"So, who is Mira when she is not Mira?" Emrys' eyes darted around, "If that makes any sense."

"Nathan is my guy name," Mira thought his awkwardness was so cute.

"Nathan." He repeated, "Nathan and Mira, those are both such beautiful names. They suit you. A handsome name for a handsome man, and a beautiful name for a beautiful woman."

Mira looked him in the eyes. Those perfect blue eyes. He was everything she ever wanted in a friend, companion, and lover: a perfect complement to her in every way.

They stood on the porch talking for the rest of the night, getting to know each other.

Mira thought he was romantic and sweet. He sincerely wanted to know about her. What she liked, what she didn't.

He asked about her favorite food, Chinese, Shrimp and Lobster Sauce to be specific. He was mining information to make the perfect date. Mira knew it, and played along. She had such strong feelings for Cyn, but since she didn't appear to be interested, she allowed herself to open up to Emrys.

"So, when can I see you again?" Emrys asked.

Mira thought for a moment. "We are getting ready for New Year's Eve, so I don't have a lot of free time right now." It hurt her to see him wilt from her words, "Why don't you meet me here for new years?"

Emrys burst back to life, "It's a date!"

Chapter 10

New Year Dawns

Harlow checked her wig in the mirror. She sat down and watched all the other queens reflexions. She brought her persona into focus in her mind. Usually, she slipped into Harlow like a comfortable sweater, but today was different.

She saw Marley laugh at something Rouge said.

Her mask slipped again. It was hard to stay in character around Marley. Harlow longed to be more direct, but around Marley she was just Shin Ki: a little boy in a dress.

She didn't like that little boy she was in high school. An outcast who was the punch line of every joke and the one who didn't know how to get out of herself. Everything was wrong, every word, every item of clothes, and unfortunately almost every friendship.

In the years since, Harlow had crafted an ideal persona, the person she would be if she could wave a magic wand and make it so. If only magic wands worked like that... Instead, she found herself more often than not stuck in the chasm between her strong persona and her frail self.

She hated feeling trapped. That's why she created Harlow. No one ever said she was cute as Shin Ki. Everybody drooled over Harlow. She was grace, beauty, humor, and fierceness personified. She learned a lot about life from playing Harlow. Harlow was a part of her.

The best parts, but the past haunted her like a Greek chorus calling her out as a fraud.

She didn't feel like a fraud. She knew that was just the voice of everyone who ever picked on her echoing in the back of her mind. Today, the echoes were louder than usual.

Who cares. She flared her nostrils and felt a fire kindle within her. She was better than all those little people who picked on her to make their own meaningless lives feel significant. She puffed out her chest and laughed.

"Go, bitch, let have," Harlow twisted her shoulders back and forth while keeping her head fixed in place. She laughed wildly and felt the mask slip on.

She bounced up onto her toes and spun around. "If we are going to do this, let's get it started. Perfection waits on no one."

The other dolls chuckled, and followed her out on the stage.

Marley demonstrated the steps for a new number they were working on. Harlow missed the name of the song. She couldn't concentrate on trivial details like that while Marley was dancing.

In her mind, Harlow heard George Michael singing Faith. She knew that wasn't the real song, but she needed to pump herself up to say what she needed to say, and that song worked better.

Harlow ran through the choreography with Rouge and Marley. She didn't miss a step. That was one benefit of falling in love with the choreographer. You watched their movements closely and burned each one in your mind.

She still didn't know what song she was dancing to, or what Rouge was saying. Neither warranted the space yet. She took some pointers from Marley, and stepped her game up further.

The spell broke.

Nathan ran onto the dance floor nearly tripping over himself. "Sorry, I'm late," he fumbled with the bags in his hands, "I needed to pick up something new for tonight, and it took longer that I thought it would."

"O, honey," Harlow said, "You own this place. You can show up whenever you want."

Nathan regained his composure and smirked at Harlow, "True, but I should set an example."

"A new frock?" Rouge raised an eyebrow. "Are you planning to make a move," She looked around to make sure she wasn't overheard, "On Cyn tonight."

Nathan blushed, "Actually," he looked away like he was caught sneaking a snack between meals, "I met someone new."

Harlow, Rouge and Marley leapt off the stage and circled him like lions on a kill.

"Who?" Rouge asked.

"His name is Emrys," Nathan fidgeted.

"That hot piece of man who was here the other night?" Harlow asked.

Nathan nodded. "He is so sweet, and not afraid to let me know he is into me."

"Unlike Cyn," Marley added, "Who you've told about Emrys, right?"

Nathan scratched an eyebrow and avoided eye contact.

"O, girl," Harlow said in a long deep tone that softened the r and l to the point they were almost an after thought.

"I know," Nathan shielded his face with a strapped paper bag containing a shoebox. "I just feel like there could be something there."

"And not with Cyn?" Rouge asked.

Nathan lowered the bag. He held his mouth closed so tightly, his top lip disappeared. "Cyn is like Paris- distant, beautiful, and charming, but I am not sure if I lose my heart there that heart will be returned."

"So," Harlow sighed as she talked, "You are willing to close the door on Cyn, who you have been doting over to try to have a relationship with this new guy?"

"I feel like there is more of a chance to build something with Emrys than with Cyn." Nathan looked almost convinced of what he was saying.

"Not every feeling should be acted upon," Harlow said.

"Yeah," Rouge grinned like the devil herself, "Sometimes, I feel like bitch slapping you when you get mopey, but I don't."

Nathan laughed.

"You don't want to mess up what you have with Cyn unless you are sure its right," Harlow said.

Rouge and Marley voiced their agreement.

"And what do I have with Cyn?" One by one, Nathan moved his stare from Harlow to Rouge to Marley.

Silence.

"You can't lose what you don't have." Nathan said.

Those words wounded Harlow. They were true and fit her feelings for Marley exactly. She was afraid of loosing a future they didn't have yet.

Harlow watched Marley closely. If they were going to be together, pronouncements and words were not going to make it happen. They needed to get closer first.

Nathan pushed through them and headed for the backstage door.

Harlow returned to the practice.

Castle ran up the steps and through the door into Wand and Weaver. He was running late.

He waved at Robin behind the bar, and rushed toward the stage door.

Cyn stood outside the cracked door, peering in.

Castle stopped.

Listening carefully, he couldn't pick up the conversation from beyond the door. He turned his attention to Cyn.

Breathe in. Breathe out. He opened himself up. He noticed every shadow, every reflexion, every trick of pattern and grain in the wood and the tile.

He ran his eyes up Cyn's body. She was nervous... Worried about something... Something the others were talking about.

There it was. It was like a pale shadow just off Cyn. A secret. Something hidden.

The first layers were easy to peel back: gender and age. So she was male, and older than she appeared, but there was something else. Something more elusive.

Castle probed the shadow for the answer.

Cyn turned around and smiled. "You're late, Oban." Her voice was silky and accused him of more than tardiness.

"I know." Castle acted like he didn't notice. "I am working on something for a friend, and I lost track of the time."

"You should be getting ready, not trying to read me." Cyn's voice grew cold.

Castle recoiled and mimed shock, "I wasn't. I just thought something was going on backstage, and didn't want to look like I was prying."

"Oh," Cyn nodded slowly. "I see."

"You are a mystery," Castle said. "The others are like an open book compared to you. You are a real mystery."

"Yeah, Curtain," Cyn laughed.

Castle understood Cyn instantly, but laughed as if he didn't. Curtain was the last Poirot novel, where the sleuth was killed by the villain.

"I should get dolled up," Castle said.

He walked up to the door and Cyn slowly stepped back.

"Smile," Cyn said as he passed, "It's New Year's Eve."

Mira clipped her earrings on. She never wanted to get them pierced. The idea had never crossed her mind. Everything Rouge, Harlow, and Marley said still rang in her ears. What would she do about Cyn. She was bound to see Emrys tonight. That could be a problem if she had feelings for Mira, but if she didn't.

Like an angel invoked in times of trouble, Cyn walked in like she heard her name being called.

Mira watched her check her flawless makeup in the mirror.

"You took your time getting into makeup tonight," Cyn said, turning her attention to Mira.

"Bought a new dress," Mira stood up. She struck a couple poses in her new black dress. The fabric was sheer with delicate red bead work that both covered and drew attention to her naughty bits before trailing off into what resembled the light of sunset reflected on a pool of dark water. It matched her red heels and wig that towered elegantly over a gold and ruby tiara.

Cyn approved with her eyes. "It was worth being late for that," she crinkled her nose, "You look like a queen ready for a night on the town."

Mira thanked her, and returned to the mirror, pretending to make some final touch ups on her look. "I just wanted you to know," her voice cracked, "I have a date coming tonight."

She watched Cyn for any hint of emotion, but she just stood there, maybe for a little bit longer than she should have if she wasn't trying to hold something in.

"Anyone I know?" Cyn asked.

"I don't think so," Mira forced herself to face Cyn, "Emrys Talson. You might have seen him the other night when he stopped in."

Cyn shook her head slowly, "I must have been busy."

Mira noticed something in her voice. She was holding something back, but what? Her voice was strained and a little forced.

"Have I upset you?" Mira asked, fearing the answer.

"Why should you have?" Cyn wasn't convincing. "It's not like we were dating or anything. We just shared a few laughs."

Before Mira could respond, Cyn walked out of the room.

Mira thought about going after her. What would she say anyway? "Well, if you hadn't been so standoffish, then I would be kissing you at midnight!" That would not go over well.

Images from the dreams she had of kissing Cyn flashed through her mind. That was the problem. They were just dreams. If Cyn had feeling, she should have acted on them before someone else did.

Mira walked out onto the dance floor. Wand and Weaver was packed. She joined the dancers, and made her way across the room. She kept an eye open for Emrys. He wasn't here yet, and for all Mira knew wouldn't even be here. Just because Mira had been counting the days, didn't mean that he had.

What would she do if he didn't come? No, that was a thought for later.

Mira busied herself helping Robin at the bar and running drinks to the tables. She did her very best to draw her attention from the clocks, but they drew her eye back over and over.

Time moved excruciatingly slow.

Every time someone entered or left, Mira glanced at the door hoping to see Emrys. Just another couple rushing off to greet in the new year more. . . privately.

Midnight approached.

Mira and the girls passed out the champaign, party hats, and noise makers of all sorts. Lady Oban checked the confetti charms and started weaving the nova effect for the moment the clock struck twelve.

There was still no sign of Emrys.

Groups divided into couples.

Mira felt so alone.

Two minutes till midnight.

The dance music wound down, replaced with an anticipatory murmur from the crowd.

One minute till midnight.

Mira knew she messed up.

The door swung open.

She turned to look.

The faery lights lit.

Emrys ran over to Mira.

"I'm sorry I'm late," he said.

"Ten!" crowd roared.

"I had something else I had to do."

"Six!"

"But I had to be here for this."

"Three! Two!"

Mira and Emrys joined in, "One!"

The Nova erupted into brilliant light.

Emrys grabbed Mira and pulled her into a kiss.

The Faery lights shattered. Sparks rained down on them.

He was so warm. His lips promising happiness and pleasure. They didn't kiss just once. They held each other in an endless moment of pure love and desire. Warmth flooded Mira. She didn't want to stop. This was where she belonged. Forever in these arms.

"Happy new year," Emrys said, pulling back slightly to free his lips from the kisses.

"Happy new year," Mira whispered into his ear.

The music thundered to life.

"I told you I would be here," Emrys said, "I hope you're not mad it took me so long."

Mira shook her head slowly, "You were right on time."

"Are we Still on for our date?" he asked.

"Of course," she said.

Mira looked around for Cyn, hoping she was alright. She couldn't find her anywhere, and sighed. She would have to patch things up with her, but that would have to wait.

Emrys grabbed her hands, "I'm sorry, but I have to get up early tomorrow." He kissed her again, "See you Wednesday."

Mira kissed him again. She wished he could stay longer, but part of her was glad he was leaving. Now that memory of their first kiss would be pristine, perfect.

Cyn checked her makeup one last time in the mirror. It was almost time for her to go on stage, and she wanted to be sure everything was perfect.

She thought a lot about what Mira said. She didn't know what to do. Mira was her first thought when she woke in the morning, and last thought before she went to bed at night.

That makes me a stalker, not a lover. Cyn thought. *I cannot allow infatuation to take over. I need to do what is best for her.*

Then she wished she knew what that was. She hoped she was doing the right thing. This was a new feelings for her. She had never felt like this for anyone, and knew that these feelings would never go away, thanks to her screw up. She had to manage them.

That makes Mira sound like an addiction. She shook her head. *She kind of is, thanks to me.* She sighed, one of those long sighs that is suppose to release frustration, and had this been over anything else, it probably would have.

She heard her cue, and walked out onto the stage to perform Meat Loaf's Out of the Frying Pan and into the Fire. She was singing, and she really felt the words.

She saw Mira watching her, and she sang the bridge directly to her. Every word came from her heart.

Lady Oban twisted and bent the light to make it look like Cyn was walking through ancient ruins. When Cyn repeatedly sang the word, "fire," torches burst to life.

Cyn pumped her life's blood into the song. The audience followed along with her. This song was everything she felt.

Her desires conflicted. She wanted so many things that could never coexist. She wanted to make good on the promise that brought her here, but that was impossible now. And she wanted to be with

Mira, but that felt like more of a pipe dream than ever. She had some reasons to hope, but she could have deluded herself into seeing what wasn't really there.

The memory of Mira in her arms made them ache. She threw them into the air and jumped up and down with the pulsing of the fire.

The other queens joined her on the stage at the end of the song, and sang along.

The audience jumped in and shouted along with them.

United in a single voice they all sang the last repetition of the chorus. The song was an anthem for the new year. It was time to make hard choices. Everyone knew it and was on board.

As they sang, they felt like a community. Together, they could walk through the fire, and no one would get hurt.

When the song ended, the crowd erupted into a loud cheer.

The soft guitar from the Lullaby broke through their cheering.

As they did every night, they performed the Lullaby to announce that Wand and Weaver was closing.

The crowd held each other and sang along with the chorus. You could tell who the regulars were.

After the song, as the crowd dispersed, Cyn walked over to Mira.

"Happy New Years, Sweetie." Cyn couldn't help but smile. It had been a long time since she truly felt a part of a community. "How do you feel about the new year?"

"I am ready to jump into the fire." Mira said, emphasizing the word fire like they had in the song.

Cyn processed that for a moment. She loved seeing Mira so happy. "Honey, I think you are already in."

Mira laughed and gave her a hug. "We all are." She said, and walked off to lock the doors.

Nathan sat in a ribbon of sunlight at the table in the sort of dining room adjacent to the living room staring at his hands. Part of him was really excited about his blossoming relationship with Emrys, and part was saddened over his relationship with Cyn. His teeth were a little sensitive from grinding them all night while he slept, so he avoided anything crunchy for breakfast or lunch.

The noon news reported another dwayyo attack over night. The body of Lauren Travers was found next to her car in a horrible state of mutilation and dismemberment. She had apparently been ripped apart, but not consumed by the beast.

It didn't make any sense. Why would any creature savage another for no apparent reason. While it wouldn't soften the horror if the beast ate her, it would at least provide a motive for the attack other than senseless violence.

He couldn't help but think of the night the beast came for him. It would have torn him to shreds if that strange night bird hadn't saved him. . . But why had it saved him and not her? That made even less sense. Something protected him specifically.

He sighed. It was just his luck to spend all his savings to start Wand and Weaver just before something like this happened. He didn't feel safe outside. He had taken to running to and from his car. If they didn't do something soon, he would have to move. He couldn't live with this constant fear looming in the recesses of his mind.

The last thing Nathan wanted to do was move again. Since he was born in Cedar Valley, Missouri, his family moved around a lot. He was in new schools constantly. They stayed in Schleyfield longer than any other place, mainly because Nathan threw such a big tantrum when they moved here. He didn't want to move anymore, but if the Dwayyo wasn't contained soon. . . It was better than the fear.

Robin's voice finally broke through.

Nathan looked up and shook off the deep thoughts, "What?"

"I said," Robin said, frustration showed in his face, posture, and voice, "Are you going to be a font of gloom all day, or do you want to share with the group?"

"I'm sorry," Nathan returned his focus to his folded hands on the table, "The news about that poor girl got me thinking, what if that had been me?"

"It wasn't!" Robin was sharp. He sat down opposite Nathan at the table. "You can't live in might have been."

"I know. That is why I was thinking about pulling up stakes and leaving."

"Monsters come in all shapes and sizes," Robin said. "If you run, you'll just find another one. You have to plant your feet in the ground and stake your claim. No one can run you out of town. You can only choose to give up."

"Then maybe I should get to work on a white flag." Nathan's shoulder's sank.

"That is one option." Robin sighed. "I have risked everything to come here. I served the Seelie Court for centuries. I played the jester, and lived the life they prescribed. Now, I want something that is my own. I'm not sure what that is. I've been the stereotype, the trickster, the motley fool, none of that fits me right now. So, I left to build a new life, despite Jack's threats."

"Has he been giving you trouble?"

"That is a polite way to put it." Robin released an anxious laugh that sounded like a cackling bird. "I endure his harassment because there isn't a better option for me right now. Sure, I could run, but he would follow me. Or I would find some other trouble elsewhere. I would rather face the demon I know, than the one I don't."

"Even if it might mean your death?" Nathan looked up and studied Robin's face carefully.

"If I am not living a life that is mine, then I am already dead."

"If you're right, then I was dead until I spoke out against the Herald." He remembered how he felt at the moment he took the podium to give his speech.

He assumed it was the thrill of public speaking or the stress of having the crowd turn against him. He was wrong. All of his senses came alive in a way he never really knew. His voice was strong. His back ached because he had straightened his posture. He had come alive.

A tear ran down his face.

"You're right," he said, or more heard himself say. He was still lost in the memories of everything that happened since that day. "I cannot let my fear get in the way of what might be an amazing experience."

Robin grinned, "It's not just you, you are living for anymore. You are the founder of Wand and Weaver. You started something there. You are responsible for your employees and clientele. Not to mention you made a pact with the Seelie Court, and if Titania thinks you are breaking it. . ." His voice trailed off ominously.

"Then we need to figure out what we can do to help the community." Nathan stood up, "I just want to finally take control of my life. I want to be free, and to help people. It is the only thing that stops the pain."

"Pain?" Robin asked.

"Of being alone."

Daniel stood outside the Sith Thyrsa Shrine. If he had come as Marley, he probably would have just walked in. Choice of persona mattered. Since he didn't, he just stood in the parking lot looking at the golden romanesque dome with its four towers, one for each of the elements. Light glimmered from the top of the water tower, and smoke fragrantly plumed from the fire tower.

He needed to see the Erythraean Sibyl. As soon as he did though, his secret would come out. She would know what he was, and his fate would literally be in her hands.

He walked up to the doors. Statues of the giants Fritha and Scildend towered on either side of the wooden doors. He felt like they scowled down at him, but he forced the thought from his mind.

The brass door knob was cold in his hand. He twisted it, opened the wooden door, and walked in.

The floors were made of unpolished stone. The phrase "se sith thara thyrsa" was inlaid in the floor in a line toward the central altar. "The path of the giants out of this world." The Old English creed was engrained in every drymann from birth. It was a covenant and the manner of life they were to follow.

Over the altar, the center of the dome opened to the sky to represent the tower of spirit in between the other four. The power invoked during services entered through there, and exited through afterwards.

Daniel walked around the outside of the large open sanctuary to a stairwell that led down to the crypt. He didn't want to keep his appointment, but he had to know if he was the cause of the Dwayyo attacks and if they could be stopped before the Ryukishi arrived. The Sibyl was his best bet to find the answers he needed.

The stairs led to a small room lit only by candle light, with a few stone benches opposite a flowing white curtain. The smell of the incense almost choked him. It was thick. Dracaena resin, commonly known as Dragon's Blood. It was a medicinal plant that some believed would maintain the health of the Sibyl as she bared her soul to the essential waves of fate surrounding her.

It was all a bit too cliche for Daniel. Just a touch of stagecraft.

He didn't wait for his name to be called. He entered through the curtain into a cavernous room. The incense hung in the air like the product of a film crew's fog machine. A single brazier in the center lit the room.

On the far side of the room, he could make out the vaguely feminine silhouette of Aimee Millar, the local Erythraean Sibyl.

Daniel felt her eyes capture him. "Greetings brother," she said in an ethereal voice.

"You call me a brother?" Daniel was skeptical. That was far from the greeting he expected.

"It isn't your fault who your mother was," the Sibyl said.

"I suppose you know why I am here?" Daniel said, still waiting for her condescension.

"Yes, brother," her voice softened, "You are not the only one who worries about the Dark Gentry. I don't want them around as much as you."

"I doubt that," Daniel scoffed. He could feel his aura mingling with hers.

Dragon spawn were all connected, and their souls reached out to one another over vast distances. Daniel always knew where the Sibyl was, and he suspected she knew as much about him. Being this close to her was uncomfortable. There was no personal space. It was like showering with a stranger. Everything was exposed.

"Are they coming?" Daniel asked.

Energy rippled through the Sibyl's aura.

"They are concerned. Lost between their duty and their desire not to lose any more of their ranks." She paused for a moment. "You know what happened last time the Dwayyo raged?"

"Several Ryukishi died at its hands." Daniel said. He paced around the room, "So they want a better plan this time around. Can't they just repeat whatever it was they did last time?"

Power surged through the air. Past and future smothered the present.

"Last time they got lucky." The tension in the air released after the Sibyl spoke. "They want to have a better plan this time."

Daniel stopped and turned his back to the Sibyl, "Am I the reason the beast returned?"

"No." The Sibyl responded immediately. "The beast is hungry for revenge, but not against our kind."

Our kind. Daniel's heart warmed towards her. "So, is there anyway we can stop it?"

The energies in the room pulled tight again. Daniel could barely breath. Oppressive heat swam with shadows of possible futures. He could feel her pain. Fate struggled against her.

"The darkness chokes on shadows." Aimee said at last. "We are in the Founder's hand, and by the hand of his betrayer will the beast be slain."

The tension broke throwing Daniel to his knees.

"The Uhtsceathan?" Daniel's blood froze. "The giants' betrayer? They. . . Were all killed, weren't they?"

"I am not sure," Aimee said, out of breath, "The future is vague. You have your words of prophecy. Please do not ask for more."

Daniel didn't understand the prophecy, but he could feel her fatigue, so he didn't push for more. The only way he could understand the prophecy made the solution worse than the problem. "By the spirits, I hope I'm wrong."

Chapter 11

To Call a Wolf

Nathan drove to the Sith Thyrsa Shrine Sunday for services, but he couldn't get out of the car. It was like his legs were turned to lead, and his heart just failed him.

He tried again Monday. He stepped out of the car, but couldn't pass the mental barrier between him and the shrine.

The next day, he forced himself to walk to the door. He paused. The Shrine used to feel like home, but now he was entering enemy territory. He wondered if his faith was based on a lie. He practiced the rituals, lived in accord with the covenant, and believed everything he was taught. . . then he was called a heretic for not hating or at least viewing with suspicion people who were born outside the faith for no fault of their own. He couldn't view someone as less just because they weren't drymenn. Those who were and didn't follow Sith Thyrsa were usually threats, but he didn't see himself as one of those.

He couldn't turn back today. He had to face his demons.

Opening the door, he walked in. The incense from the morning services filled the air with spicy wonder. The light shown through the eye in the dome. He wanted more than anything to feel at ease. He wanted to cry. The tears refused to ease his spirit.

He knelt and bowed toward the altar, as was his custom, and tried to pray. The words resisted like the tears.

He heard Curate Hugh McDonough walking through the sanctuary. The sound of his prayer beads clacking together was distinctive.

"Father," Nathan said as he stood up.

Curate Hugh McDonough was a kind old man, the local curate for around forty years. He looked like a classic grandfather with his short snow white hair and wire rimmed glasses. He wore the black cassock traditional to the curate. The average person would easily confuse him for a catholic priest unless they noticed the lack of a collar and the blue detailing.

"Nathan," Hugh smiled and threw open his arms. "It has been a while since I've seen you. I heard you were back in town." His voice was comforting.

Nathan walked over to him and gave him a hug, "I'm sure you have heard a lot of things about me."

Hugh nodded, "I was surprised you haven't joined us for services."

"That's not easy." Nathan shifted around. "After what happened with Paul. . ."

"Paul is an idiot," Hugh chuckled, "I told Herald Maughan that he should be defrocked for his actions, and Lydia agreed. She plans to bring him up on charges at the next conclave. After the troubles with the Thulites in the the '30's and '40's, there are rules about that sort of thing."

Nathan grinned, "Do you think he will be defrocked?"

"Leoma thara Mennisca clearly states everything that you said, and it imposes penalties on curates who discriminate on the basis of the covenant or possession of magic. You struck a nerve in him, and he violated canon law." Hugh wrapped an arm around Nathan. "I told you to go to Blackwood Abbey, but you wouldn't listen."

"I know. I actually came to ask you about the Dwayyo."

Hugh pulled his arm back. "Come to my office."

Nathan watched the old curate look around nervously. He followed him to his office, and sat in the chair offered to him.

Hugh closed the door, and sat across from him. "That is a touchy subject, child. What do you want to know?"

"I know this has happened before. How did they stop it last time?" Nathan pulled a small notebook and a pen out of his pocket.

"No one knows. The Ryukishi handled it. Several of them died before they banished the beast from our world."

"Who or what summoned it last time?"

Hugh swallowed hard. "We really don't know. It was the late sixties. Most people thought at the time that it was an accident. A group of drymann on acid or some other drugs called it by accident."

"Why?"

"A group of campers were the first recorded victims. People just assumed they summoned it."

Nathan jotted down a few notes. "What is the Dwayyo?"

Hugh leaned forward, "The Dwayyo is the Cetus of the woods." He leaned back in his chair.

Cetus was a sea serpent. Nathan thought. It didn't make sense.

"He is like a flock of man eating sheep, or Cerberus protecting Persephone's beauty." Hugh added.

Nathan knew the curate was trying to tell him something he couldn't say outright, but he couldn't put it together. He wasn't that familiar with Greek mythology, and was surprised Hugh was talking in some kind of code.

"Is there any way to defend against the Dwayyo?" Nathan asked.

"No."

"Were there any patterns in the attacks last time?"

"No."

At least those were clear answers. They weren't very helpful, but they were answers.

Nathan wrote everything Hugh said in his notebook, and stared at it for a while. One question burned in his mind, "Do you know why the Dwayyo is here?"

Hugh pursed his lips and sighed. The sigh was almost imperceptible, but it was there. "It is a sign that darkness longs to conquer light."

That was a yes. Nathan wondered if asking these questions put Hugh in danger. He politely excused himself and left the shrine.

Harlow checked her makeup in the mirror, and listened to Marley and Rouge talking. Well, she wanted to listen, but couldn't muster enough interest to pay attention to the words.

She reexamined herself in the mirror.

A beautiful Korean woman who belonged in a Marlene Dietrich film looked back. She loved the transformation, and spent a moment focusing on her real male face. There was something even beyond magic involved in applying the makeup.

She felt herself slipping into character as each layer built upon the last. She thought about the fine line between her masculinity and femininity. Out of drag, she felt a little bit naked because the world could see her as she is.

Once painted and dressed, she felt free. The mask was part of it, but not the whole. It wasn't a costume or a character. It was a persona she could inhabit. When she dolled herself up, she allowed herself to choose who she wanted to be and how she wanted to act. She allowed herself to be free. If only she could take more of that into her everyday life, without the makeup.

She looked at Marley through the mirror, and smiled.

Her heart warmed. This was her moment. The other queens were heading out to the front of house.

"Marley," Harlow called out, pretending to check for makeup lines on her chin and neck, "Could I have a moment?"

"Of course," Marley said without her trademark bubbliness.

Harlow swiveled around, "Is everything alright?

Marley stood silent for a moment, "I suppose. I just have a lot on my mind."

"I'm sure. With all the choreography and such, and everything else going on."

Marley stiffened a bit.

"I mean in the news. That beast roaming around. We're lucky none of us have been killed." Harlow wondered if Marley was as worried as she was.

"Am I reading too much into it, or does there seem to be a message in the attacks." Marley's voice was more serious than Harlow had ever heard it.

"What kind of message?"

"All of the attacks have been near fences or on the edge of the forest. The first attack was on a flock of sheep between a fence and the woods. That sounds like a sacrifice to me."

Harlow didn't know what to make of what Marley was saying. "It seems like coincidence to me. I mean what better place to ambush or corner someone."

Marley sighed. "I suppose you're right." She shook her head and looked into Harlow's eyes with a forced smile, "I'm sorry, what did you want to talk about?"

"Actually," Harlow rallied her nerve, "It was related to the Dwayyo. I am kind of afraid to be alone right now. Do you mind if I stay with you?"

Marley raised an eyebrow.

Harlow blushed, exaggerating her body language since she doubted Marley could tell through her makeup, "Not like that... Exactly. I just don't want to be alone right now, and I don't want you to be alone either."

Marley smiled, "I suppose there is safety in numbers. Sure."

Daniel's first night with his new roommate went well. He felt bad that Harlow slept on the couch, but he didn't seem to mind.

The hardest part was finding time to practice some of the secret keeper arts that Castle taught him. They didn't come naturally to him.

He'd never spent time noticing the things his eye was use to ignoring: the qualities of shadows, the sources of light, the random patterns in wood grain, brick, tile, and carpet. It tired his eyes more than he thought it would.

Several times, Castle reinforced the importance of seeing the minutia and the big picture simultaneously.

Since Harlow wanted to talk for a while after they got home, he used that as an opportunity to study the quality of his and Harlow's voices, and how the tones affected his perception of the room.

He found it interesting that every time Harlow spoke the room became slightly rosy. He made a mental note to ask Castle about that during their next lesson.

The next morning, the light was icier than the air. He had to run a few errands in town and noticed the nearly imperceptible sneers, smiles, and lost expressions that covered people's faces when they didn't realize that they were revealing their real feelings.

It made his interactions with people a little harder since he was seeing hints at the hidden meanings behind their words and expressions. He could see how this art was useful and a burden. He also understood why the art was called secret keeping.

A few times, he reacted to the unconscious hints he was seeing, and the people acted like he was strange. The art had to be kept secret because it let you know too much.

Castle's quirks were a lot less quirky to him now.

As he drove to Wand and Weaver that afternoon, Daniel thought about all the secrets he was learning to uncover, and the ones he was keeping.

He thought about telling Nathan what he was, but he was afraid it would just endanger him if the truth got out. He had to tell him the Sibyl's prophecy. He hoped Nathan would understand.

After parking in the employee area of the parking lot, he get out of the car. Something was off... different.

He looked around, trying to see what he shouldn't notice.

There it was. On the ground and the asphalt, faint trails scintillated like light randomly hitting glitter. As he looked around, he noticed five of these golden rainbow trails leading off into the woods behind Wand and Weaver.

Some of the trails looked like a footpath, but others were larger.

He didn't understand what it meant, and filed it away to ask Castle about it later.

Daniel headed in, refocusing himself on sharing the prophecy. He waved at Robin as he walked through the bar. He noticed Nathan going into his office, and walked for the door.

"Hey, Mira," he said before Nathan could close the door.

He looked up from whatever was in his hands, "Hey Daniel."

"I need to talk to you in your office of a moment."

Nathan beckoned him in. He walked over to his desk and sat down, "Have you given anymore thought to what we are going to do for the Wolf Moon if the Dwayyo is still out and about?"

Daniel closed the door behind himself. "Not really, but that is over a month away, so we have time to figure it out."

"True, what did you want?"

Sitting down, Daniel forced his shoulders to relax. "I went to the Sibyl on New Years."

The smile faded from Nathan. "What did she say?"

"Well," Daniel reconsidered telling him, but needed to tell him. "She said, The darkness chokes on shadows. We are in the Founder's hand, and by the hand of his betrayer will the beast be slain."

"What the does that mean? Did she give you an interpretation?"

Daniel shook his head. "I was hoping you would have an idea."

Nathan melted like wax under an oppressive light. "I think I might know what it means."

"Care to share?" Daniel asked, already knowing the answer.

"I can't. I think it means you need to focus on keeping yourself safe right now."

Chapter 12

Voice in the Flames

Nathan couldn't stop thinking about the Sibyl's prophecy to him and the new one to Daniel. He told Robin and Rouge, but they just wrote it off. They couldn't feel the sting of the words like he did.

Herald Paul Kincaid proclaiming him a heretic rang like thunder in his mind. Had he really threatened the covenant with the giants? Was he the betrayer of the founder? If the Herald was right, he was.

He had to know one way or the other.

He'd spent enough time at the seminary to know the call of the giants, and resolved to go to South Mountain and ask them.

Rouge thought he was an idiot, and Robin couldn't understand why he cared so much, but they wouldn't let him go alone.

Sunday afternoon, they loaded into Nathan's Stirling Regen with Rouge in the back seat, and headed for Fort Richie.

Robin fidgeted in his seat. "Are you sure you don't want me to zap us there?"

Nathan and Rouge laughed.

"I'm sure," Nathan said. "I've traveled with you before, and it made me sick. Too much whirling around for my taste."

"Besides," Rouge added, "I don't want to mess my hair up."

Robin scowled at each of them in turn, then crossed his arms and pouted. "Don't you Drymenn have a better means of travel than a steam car?"

Nathan smiled, "Yes, we have airships and trains." He laughed. "There are incantations and travel charms, but half the fun is the journey."

"If you say so." Robin said.

"Have you thought what your are going to say to the Royer Lake Moura?" Rouge asked.

"Other than let me pass?" Nathan turned onto the Waynesboro Pike. "Not really. I am more concerned about what I am going to do if the giants refuse to talk to me."

Robin rolled his eyes, "Why in the name of this tiny blue planet wouldn't they talk to you? You have the right to ask for an audience. Don't you?"

"Technically," Rouge said. "Any drymann has the right to request an audience with the giants, but they have the right to refuse the call or send an emissary. I am more curious why you picked Quirauk Mountain instead of Lambs Knoll or Fox's Gap, or better still Crampton's Gap."

"I thought about Crampton's Gap, but Quirauk is treaty territory. The Sith Thyrsa have a treaty with the Wrecca to guard the mountain. I figured it was our best place to find a giant."

"Makes sense to me," Robin said.

"I just think Gathland is a lot more fun, and easy. No mountain to climb." Rouge grinned, "I haven't gone through the arch in a while."

Raise your Glass by Pink came on the radio, and Nathan turned it up. They sang along to the radio the rest of the way to Fort Richie.

As he drove down MacAfee Hill Rd, Nathan saw the iron and stone gate coming up on his right, and said, "Moura, acythe thaet infaer!" He waved his hand toward the gate, which rippled and tore down the middle like a sheet of paper. None of the other motorists could see it.

The gate now had three arches. He turned into the middle lane, and felt a chill as he passed through the arch onto the hidden road.

He pulled into an empty parking lot next to the small Royer Lake.

A few small bushes and smattering of trees ringed the near shore of the lake, and across the water stood the tree covered summit of Quirauk with the wrecca broadcast towers atop the mountain.

They got out of the car.

The water rose up to greet them, splashing over the shore and rising into a beautiful, young woman with long, flowing, silver hair. The water rolled and rushed around her body. It looked like shimmering white samite with crystal blue swirls. An icy breeze gushed from the Moura.

"Hold, drymenn and fae!" The moura's voice thundered. "Why are you here uninvited?" She scowled at them.

Nathan stepped forward, and stood up straight. "I am here to see the giants."

"You invoke the covenant?" The moura sounded skeptical. "Then why is the fae here? They have no part in the covenant."

"He is here for moral support."

The moura glared at Robin. "If I guide you to Ealh Waere, the fae must refrain from using magic."

Robin recoiled, but swallowed his venom.

The moura turned to Rouge. "If I guide you to Ealh Waere, the covenant must be followed."

Rouge furrowed his brow.

The moura looked down at Nathan. "If I guide you to Ealh Waere, you must call the giants."

Without waiting for any of them to respond, the moura turned to face Quirauk Mountain, and began walking toward the water. As she walked, the white samite under the water elongated into a train.

Nathan didn't know what he was supposed to do. He rushed to follow her and heard Robin and Rouge behind him.

When he stepped onto the moura's train, he almost fell back. It was solid.

Standing on the train, the three followed the moura across the lake. Nathan felt sorry for the wrecca who lived on its shore who had no idea how large and beautiful the rich blue lake really was. Then he looked up at Quirauk.

The shadow of Ealh Waere loomed over the top of the mountain in silent stone splendor. The standing stones stood as a silent witness to the covenant. He looked back to the wrecca town and wondered if it was fair to hide such beauty from their eyes.

As they approached the far shore, he noticed the long stairway carved out of the rock that snaked its way up to Ealh Waere.

The moura stepped out of the lake onto the landing. When their feet were over the stone, her train melted back into lake water.

It was dusk by the time they finished climbing the steps to Ealh Waere.

The large gray stones stood in a silent circle around an altar and fire pit. Tall trees joined the stones as guardians around the top of the mountain.

By the time they gathered wood for the fire, the sun had set.

Nathan built the fire, and sat in its warm glow. He began to recite the call of the giants. His voice was weak at first. He focused on the proper emphasis of each word. He knew he had the right to call on them, but he had never met a giant before. He didn't know how they would react to him. He didn't even know if they would speak english.

He continued the chant. He focused on his yearning. He needed answers, and he felt that they were the only source.

He thought about the Dwayyo, and how he hadn't considered whether or not they would be safe out here all night. At least his friends were with him. If worse came to worst, maybe he and Rouge could hold it off long enough for Robin to get them to safety.

Besides, he was on holy land in a treaty protected area. Surely, they would be safe here of all places.

He heard something behind him.

Turning around without breaking the chant, he saw that Robin and Rouge had fallen asleep.

His spirit deflated a bit.

Nathan wished his friends could have waited with him, but Rouge didn't know that chant, and he knew Robin was not used to traveling like they did.

Returning his focus to the fire, he poured his disappointment and fear into the call.

At least they wouldn't hear the answer if he was to blame for all their problems.

Something was strange in the air. The smell of the wood smoke mingled with the scent of something more exotic, something almost intoxicating.

The air was calm, still.

The night birds and insects were quiet.

Something rustled in the woods to his right.

A downed tree snapped to his left.

Nathan's muscles turned to stone.

On the edge of the firelight two giants stepped out of the shadows. They were three times the size of the average man, and different.

Their flesh was not like skin. It was rougher, almost like compacted soil.

Nathan couldn't tell if their hair was matted into dreads or if they had vines for hair.

Their faces were etched with concern, ancient and withered. Their eyes were rich and full like a deer. Rippling muscles defined their bare chest and stomach. They wore rough leggings made out of leather or maybe some kind of plant. The ribs and veins on the fabric made it hard to tell.

They stood like sentinels on either side of the fire and stared down at Nathan.

Nathan prostrated before them.

"Poor child," one of them said. His voice boomed like falling boulders. "Look at us. We are not so frightful as to harm you."

Lifting his head, Nathan took in the enormity of their size. He was surprised how thin they where.

"Why have you come?" The one on his right asked.

Nathan cleared his throat. "I have been accused of breaking the covenant by one of your Heralds, and now a beast stalks the county."

"We know," said the one on the left.

"You are quite brave to come to us," the other said. "The night is dangerous for your kind."

Tears broke from Nathan's eyes, and he collapsed under their weight. "I believed you would hear me. I've always believed in your grace." He sobbed. "It kills me to think I have betrayed you."

The two giants sprinkled some powder into the fire. The flames rose high above their heads.

Within the fire a face came forward.

Nathan looked into its eyes, and felt ice water splash on his heart. It was Fritha. The writer of the covenant. He knew it in his bones. This was one of the founders.

"Poor child," Fritha's voice blew sparks from the pyre. "We have felt your anguish. None of our kind missed your pain. We are the children of the soil, young child of the sun. We know the cares and concerns of all who love our mother."

Nathan froze. He didn't know if he faced judgement or absolution. He could feel the presence of the giants unlike anything else in his life.

"The blasphemer has treated you poorly," Fritha said. "We carried the drymenn from the world of Unsotha to preserve magic. The wrecca would have killed us all. We never meant to separate the worlds. The Sith Thyrsa and the Sith Unsotha need each other."

It was hard for Nathan to take it all in. "What about the Herald? The Dwayyo?"

Fritha dissolved back into the fire.

The two giants nodded.

The giant on the right said, "The founder has said all that he can or will. Sleep here. The danger is close. We will stand guard over you."

"But I had more questions!" Nathan pleaded.

He continued to ask about the Dwayyo and the Herald for while, but the giants never spoke again.

He laid down by one of the standing stones, mulling over Fritha's words until he drifted off to sleep.

Pain.

Robin jumped up from a sound sleep.

Crack. Pain.

He turned toward the impact.

Through the low light of the campfire, he could make out a figure standing on the edge of the stone circle.

He looked around.

Nathan was asleep near one of the stones.

Rouge slept not far from him.

The backs of what had to be two giants stood by the fire.

Opposite them, a dark figure threw another rock at him.

Robin rolled out of the way.

The shadow cocked its head to the side, then looked up.

Robin followed its gaze and saw another figure sitting atop one of the standing stones.

"O Robin," Jack's familiar voice broke the silence.

Robin hopped to his feet. "What are you doing here?"

"We could ask you the same thing." Jack stepped into the light.

"You know we can't use our magic here."

Jack raised an eyebrow. "Do you think I want war?" He laughed. "That's why I threw the stone at you." He grinned. "Are you ready to come home? It is safer there."

"Safer?" Robin asked. "Did you release the Dwayyo?"

Jack looked up at the silhouette top the standing stone, "I think our friend, Robin, thinks he's too good for the Seelie."

"Who are you taking to?" Robin asked.

"Maybe he would rather be mortal." Jack said to the shadow.

"I just want a life of my own for a while." Robin strained his eyes to see who was atop the standing stone. "You did call it, didn't you?"

Jack returned his attention to Robin, "We didn't release the Dwayyo," he screwed up his face like he thought Robin was stupid to ask the question. "We do wonder if you might not be safer in Elphame. Our worlds are separate for a reason."

Robin grimaced, "What are you up to Jack?"

Jack turned to the shadow on the stone, "Looks like he's not coming with us."

The shadow leapt off the stone into darkness of the forest.

Jack slowly walked into the inky black night.

Castle sat in lotus position in his room, silhouetted by the warm, flickering light of the candles set in a semicircle around him. Motionless as a statue in an ancient temple, his breathing was so slow his chest didn't appear to move.

His eyes relaxed into the luminous halo. The flicker twisted the shadows through the light. Changes rippled through the air, elusive but close.

The room surged with energy, tingling his skin.

He turned his attention from the world around him to the wide, shallow alabaster bowl of water nestled between the candles.

Light danced through the delicate stone work. The striations moved like waves. Light surrounded the laver, peaking through the translucent stone illuminating the ripples in the water.

Castle focused all his energy.

The shadows scurried playfully around the room.

"Cyn," He breathed the word onto the water. He knew she was hiding something important, maybe even dangerous.

Pouring his desire to know the secret down his arm, he waved his hand over the water. The desire dripped like a light rain into the bowl. The water rippled.

Castle watched the patterns of light and shadow, seeking out the meaning behind them.

His eyes opened wide.

Jumping back, he flipped over the bowl.

The water dowsed the candles.

The room dimmed.

"It can't be..."

Chapter 13

To Tell the Truth

Nathan couldn't help but notice how quiet Robin was on the drive home. He told them what the giants said, and only Rouge reacted. Robin just nodded slowly.

It was unusual to see a fairy so quiet, but Nathan didn't want to push. He knew he would open up when he was ready.

As they approached the house, Nathan saw Emrys' car in the driveway.

He pulled in.

Robin and Rouge hopped out.

Getting out of the car, Nathan smiled at Emrys and waved.

Emrys met him halfway to the door.

They hugged.

Nathan savored Emrys' warmth against his body. He held on longer than he probably should have, but in his arms he felt safe.

"Is everything alright?" Emrys asked.

"Of course," Nathan let himself slip out of the embrace, "I just had an intense night."

"And they cleared your conscience."

Nathan nodded.

"I told you, you were innocent." Emrys' face beamed with pride.

Everything about Emrys made Nathan love him more. The tone of his voice. His smile. Especially his eyes. They were old, and knowing, and lit up every time their gaze met.

"I was going into town to pick up some things," Nathan said. "Would you like to come with me? We could grab some lunch."

"It's a date," Emrys said.

They walked back to the car and got in. Nathan pulled out of the driveway and headed toward town.

"So what are we picking up?" Emrys asked.

"I thought I would buy some Aconite to give away at Wand and Weaver."

Emrys gazed out the window, "Hoping that a little Wolf's Bane will live up to its name, eh."

"Well, can you think of anything else that might help?"

Emrys sighed, "No. Like everyone else in town, I've looked into it. There is something strange about all this."

"What do you mean?" Nathan said as he parked the car on the street near Herbaceous Splendour.

"Last time, the Dwayyo killed someone every night it was loose. People were found torn apart all over the county." An undertow of sorrow haunted his words. "This time, it killed some sheep, but so far, only one person. It has been seen along the road, but it hasn't attacked anyone."

Nathan turned off the Stirling engine, "It attacked me."

"What?" Emrys grabbed Nathan's hand. "Why didn't you tell me?"

"Because," Nathan was surprised by the even tone in Emrys' voice. He was a rock. "Because I knew you were the type that would have suited up and gone hunting."

Emrys squeezed Nathan's hand, "You're probably right. You know I won't let anything bad happen to you."

"I know." Nathan freed his hand and unbuckled his seatbelt. "Do you think giving away aconite is enough of a gesture." He sighed. "It probably won't do much if anything."

"It'll make them feel better." Emrys said. "Sometimes a token of security is as good as the real thing. People lock their doors and feel safe. Any criminal desiring entry can still get in. Life is dangerous. We all have many tokens and charms to make us feel safe."

Nathan palmed the protection charm he wore around his neck and rolled his fingers around its edges. "Maybe we should look for some other charms too. We can give them away as rewards for... I don't know, Daniel will think of something."

Cyn stood on the porch of Wand and Weaver. She wanted to go inside, it was almost time for work, but too much was on her mind. She didn't know what to do.

She wanted to talk to Nathan Saturday night, but she didn't have the nerve. She spent the last two day debating what to do. She wanted with every fiber of her being to tell him the truth yesterday, but he was too cozy with Emrys.

Nathan needed to know the truth. Why she came to Schleyfield. What she came to do. How she tried to poison him, and how she couldn't go through with it.

Cyn sighed and began pacing.

Would Nathan understand? She knew that was the root of all her fear. If she let the truth come out of her mouth... Nathan would hate her. That was clear. She couldn't tell him.

She closed her eyes and grabbed onto the railing.

Nathan had to know.

She had to remember the lessons of her life. Emotions get in the way. They cause pain and misery. That is all they do. Every time she let someone get close to her, one of them got hurt.

"All I do is cause pain," she muttered under her breath.

When you intentionally live a lie, how do you start to tell the truth. In her long life, she had only ever told five people her real name out of fear it would be used against her.

Nathan pulled into parking lot.

Ice pumped through Cyn's veins.

Now was the time. *If I don't tell him now, it will only be worse later.*

Cyn walked down the few steps and over to Nathan like a prisoner on their way to the gallows.

"It's beautiful this afternoon," Nathan said as he got out of his car, and headed for the trunk. "Can you help me carry these in?"

She couldn't even look into the open trunk.

"I need to talk to you." She said.

"You're not quitting are you?" Nathan looked up from the boxes in the trunk.

Cyn shook her head. "No. Well. That depends."

"What is it?" Nathan leaned against his car's bumper. "Are you upset I've been spending so much time with Emrys? I mean, I just thought you weren't interested. I mean, with us working together and all."

Emrys. Damnable Emrys. The name sank into her heart like a dragon's claw.

"I have something to tell you." Cyn said.

Nathan looked concerned.

Cyn hated that look. It meant she was causing pain. She didn't want to ever cause Nathan pain. She cursed the poison in her veins that she accidentally drank. She knew she needed to say it fast. Get it out there and reap the consequences.

"Nathan," she said. "I have something I need to tell you." The words clung to the back of her throat like a damned soul to life.

"What is it, sweetie," Nathan reached out to comfort Cyn.

Cyn pulled back.

Comfort was the last thing she wanted. She was about to admit the worst secret she ever kept.

The words betrayed her. They refused to be spoken.

"I'm sorry," Nathan said, "I need to get the aconite in, and I still need to get dressed for tonight. I hate to ask, but can this wait."

"Sure."

Cyn hated herself. That word leapt from her mouth without even asking if it could, but the truth refused to admit the possibility of words.

Castle arrived late, and rushed into the dressing room. He quickly dressed and applied makeup. Invoking a few protection and alert charms, now she could feel Cyn's presence and proximity.

Lady Oban laced up her red leather cuffs, then her red leather boots. She checked her outfit in the three way mirror. She looked like a samurai who was a lady in waiting to the queen of hearts, or a Marie Antoinette dressed for battle.

She hoped the fight wouldn't come, but after what she learned, she couldn't risk anything.

She'd spent the last two days trying to figure out what to do. Should she tell Nathan or Cyn? Should she keep quiet? The questions still burned in her mind.

Something was strange about the whole thing. She wasn't able to figure out what caused her scrying bowl to explode, or what blew out the candles. Cyn might have felt her eyes and intervened. In which case, Oban was in grave danger.

There was some strangeness to the revelation. She knew what Cyn was, and how dangerous she was. She even knew why Cyn came to town, but there was a turbulent peace in the vision that she couldn't understand. It could have meant anything. It felt important... portentous.

She had to tell Cyn what she knew and try to find out what that last hidden point was.

Oban kept an eye on Cyn all night. It was a Tuesday, so Wand and Weaver wasn't too busy so it wasn't all that hard to do.

Marley pulled her aside at one point to tell her how her secret keeper practice was going. Oban knew she was short with her, but she was sad that she brought Marley into her world.

The burden of a secret keeper was a nearly insatiable curiosity. She often thought about Pandora, the legendary first secret keeper and how sad her life was, and Cassandra and Tiresias. She couldn't think of a secret keeper that had a happy life.

That was the price of knowing.

Oban helped with clean up after Wand and Weaver closed.

Everyone seemed to be distracted by something, and her something was about to exit through the back.

She chased after Cyn, and caught up to her just outside of the back door. No one else used the back exit, so she knew this was the time for her to ask her questions without endangering anyone.

"Hey Cyn," Oban called out. Her heels clacked on the asphalt as she rushed up to Cyn.

Cyn turned around slowly, "Yes, Oban?" Her voice guarded any emotion from showing. "Did you write your letter yet?"

Oban knew that was a reference to the end of Curtain, a not so veiled threat. "I'd hoped it wouldn't come to that."

"Had you." The silver ring in Cyn's black on black eyes shimmered.

"Yes," Oban hesitated for a moment. She wanted to abandon her plan with every fiber of her being, but she pushed herself forward. "I scried about you Sunday."

"That was you?" Cyn took in a long, slow breath. The lights dimmed.

"I know who and what you are." Oban pushed the words out of her mouth. "And I know why you are here."

"Do you. Well. That is a problem."

"I also know there is something else going on. I just don't understand, how long do you think you can hide this from Mira?"

"As long as I have to."

Oban felt a conflict in Cyn, but couldn't put words to it. "Nathan needs to know. If you don't tell him. I will."

"Will you?" Cyn sneered. Her eyes darkened. "I am afraid I cannot allow that."

Shadows twisted from her hands and lashed around Oban's throat like a whip.

"You really should have listened to me."

Chapter 14

Lost in Shadows

Nathan arrived at Wand and Weaver early the next morning to discuss the weekend with Daniel. They worked out the musical numbers, and some drink specials they wanted Robin to add to the menu.

About twenty minutes before they opened the doors, Daniel gathered the Queens and Robin together to clue them in on the plan.

Nathan came out and greeted everyone... Not everyone. Lady Oban was missing.

"Where is Oban?" Nathan asked.

"Not here." Cyn answered.

"That's obvious," Nathan sighed, "Anyone call him to see if he's running late?"

"On it," Daniel said, slipping into Nathan's office.

Nathan was close to Castle from his time in Philadelphia. He wasn't the type of person to ever be late, especially not without calling. Concern pricked his skin.

Daniel exited the office. "He didn't answer."

The cold points pierced Nathan to the bone. "Hopefully, he just lost track of time, and will be in after while. He's not missing until tomorrow."

"I'd like to go to his apartment," Daniel said, "Make sure he's not sick or hurt."

"Good idea," Nathan replied. "Just get back as soon as possible. Wednesdays are a wild card, and we don't want to be two down."

Daniel nodded and headed for his car.

Daniel ran up the stairs to Castles' apartment.

He knocked on the door.

Nothing.

He banged on the door.

Nothing.

He reached into his pocket and pulled out the key Castle had given him so he would always have access to the sanctum.

The lock clicked.

Daniel pushed the door open. The scent of stale incense lingered in the air. It was old. He hadn't been home all night. He hadn't performed his evening or morning rites.

All the lights were off. The room was cloaked in inky black shadows.

Daniel forced his mind to focus on the sketchy lines in the shadows. He could see the outline of Castle leaving for work the day before.

He pressed his focus back in time.

Castle had sat in front of his altar meditating. Daniel could sense the yearning for meaning on the spent candles.

Daniel couldn't sense him in the kitchen, at least not within the last forty-eight hours. He could feel his presence back in his room.

He saw Castle jumping back and flipping over the bowl... a bowl of water as power erupted from the laver. The laver shattered, splashing water on the the circle of candles blowing them out.

Fear pervaded the room. Daniel struggled to hold onto the vision. He had to know what Castle was doing. The images slipped, then faded back into the shadows.

Daniel tried to bring it back, but the secrets were elusive. He wasn't strong enough with the art to force them from the darkness.

Walking slowly to the door, he whispered Castle's name in the hushed tones he'd been taught. If he did it right, Castle would hear the call and respond.

He listened to the silence carefully for a response.

Nothing.

A faint breath tickled his ears.

Someone was talking about him in secret, but he couldn't make out if it was Castle or someone else.

Daniel wondered if his father had something to do with Castle's disappearance, or worse, his mother. If they caught word of what he and Castle were trying to do...

He shook the idea out of his head. If either or both of his parents were involved, they would have collected him. That didn't make sense.

His shoulders dipped as he left and locked the apartment.

Walking down the stairs, he wished he could think of another place to look, or that he would hear Castle whisper back on the wind.

Daniel drove back to Wand and Weaver. It was still early, but there were a few cars in the parking lot.

He smiled at the aconite hung over the doors and windows, and hoped it was enough to keep the Dwayyo at bay.

As he made his way back to the makeup room, he waved at a few regulars. Nathan sat in front of one of the mirrors with very little makeup on.

"I would have thought you would have been kitted out by now," Daniel said. He washed his face at the sink in the back of the room.

"So," Nathan's voice was soft, "No sign of Castle at his apartment?"

Daniel shook his head as he dried off, "He's a fighter. I'm sure he's alright." The lie tasted bitter.

"What if the Dwayyo got him?"

The idea filled the room, almost squelching the lights.

"Then someone should have found a body." Daniel wasn't sure of the words, but they gave him a little hope that Castle was busy with something. "If we don't get rid of the Dwayyo soon," he continued. "They are going to send a Ryukishi to fix it. No one wants that."

Nathan sighed, "You are the sixth person to say something like that to me."

Daniel winced at the thought. "Trust me. They have taken notice. It is only a matter of time before one comes. That is the last thing I... we need."

They finished getting into drag in silence.

It was a busy night.

Marley was happy for the distraction. It kept her from worrying.

At the end of the evening, as everyone but Cyn was washing down. Rouge pulled Marley aside, and asked her out on a date.

Marley smiled for bit longer than she wanted to. "With everything else going on, I would love a brief oasis away from it."

Rouge practically skipped away.

Marley sank into the hope for a fun night out saturday night with Rouge.

Cyn knew her time was limited, but there was no good way out. She wanted to leave. Just pick up and go like she had so many times before. She wanted to blame the poison, but she knew it was more than that.

The poison only caused infatuation. At best it drove the victim to obsession. She actually had feelings.

It wasn't fair.

Cyn had been a strong loner all her life. She had never felt compassion for anyone, much less love. She hated it.

All the way to Wand and Weaver, she thought about what she wanted to do. She was jealous of Emrys and Nathan's relationship. She hated it. The weakness, the vulnerability, the tenderness. It was disgusting.

People were to be used and thrown away.

She wanted to protect Nathan. She couldn't leave until Nathan was safe, at least from the threats that he currently faced.

When she walked into the makeup room, Nathan was talking to Rouge about Oban.

That damn witch, Cyn thought.

Nathan had gone to the authorities to report Oban missing. Since there were no leads, they weren't optimistic.

She got better than she deserved, Cyn thought.

Cyn waited for Nathan to head for his mirror to get ready. She walked up behind him and asked, "So, hun, what are you doing this weekend?"

"I have a date with Emrys on Sunday." Nathan beamed.

"It sounds like he makes you happy."

Nathan swiveled around to face her. "Honestly, he does. Does that upset you?"

"Should it?"

Nathan narrowed his eyes. "O, I thought... Well..."

"That I had feelings for you?" Cyn weighed and measured her words, "You know I would do anything for you. I keep my word. And even though it is anathema to my nature, I think you are starting something special here."

Nathan looked down, "That is not an answer."

"What do you want me to say? You already found what you are looking for in Emrys. I know that, and so do you. You like the doting, saccharine, romantic lead."

"What?"

"Emrys is your Sandra Bullock, Reese Witherspoon romantic comedy inspired, perfect man. Just don't forget, this is Broken Hearts Club, not Legally Blond."

"What? Yes, I want romance, but not a cardboard cutout relationship?"

"Are you sure?" Cyn asked, "You know every relationship starts in pure fantasy, and Emrys is a fantasy to you. You need to root yourself in something real."

Daniel took Rouge to Mortal Trust/Faerie Dust in Baltimore for their date. It was a part restaurant, part club themed in the conflicting styles of the Ryukishi and the Fey.

They had dinner and danced for awhile.

Daniel had a good time, and hoped he hadn't ruined Rouge's night. He was distracted by the turmoil at Wand and Weaver. He tried to give in to the atmosphere, and just have a good time.

For the first time, he felt at home at a Ryukishi themed anything. He knew MT/FD was a safe space. Many Erythrai came in after hours to relax, so he wouldn't stand out.

He had a wonderful time. He was surprised how much he and Rouge had in common. They both loved Beauty and the Beast and Dark Wave music. They even had similar taste in drinks.

They talked most of the night.

In the car on the drive home, Rouge was unusually quiet.

"Did I talk you out?" Daniel asked.

"No," Rouge blushed, "I just had such a good time, I was afraid I'd mess it up. No words. No drama."

Daniel laughed. "Girl, I work with you. I already know all of your crazy, and I said yes to the date. Don't disappoint me now."

Rouge smiled. "I know. On that note, I should probably apologize for being such a bad dancer."

"You are not a bad dancer. You just need more attention and rehearsal than most."

"I hope you don't mind me asking this," Rouge looked out the window, "I was surprised you agreed to go out with me. You had been spending so much time with Oban lately. I thought, well, that maybe the two of you were..."

"Oh, no." Daniel took exit 53B off I-70, "He has been teaching me some things."

"You want to be a secret keeper?" Rouge turned to look at Daniel.

"Not exactly." Daniel forced himself not to tell Rouge everything. He was surprised by the amount of trust Rouge earned. "I am just interested in the art of illusion."

That killed the conversation.

Daniel hoped he hadn't scared Rouge off. He knew the stigma attached to the secret keepers, and thought that if Rouge couldn't accept that, then he would never accept him as a hanryu.

He turned off onto 26, then took the Moura's exit into Schleyfield, on his way to the house Rouge shared with Nathan and Robin.

As he pulled into the driveway, he noticed that lights in the living room were still on. Robin looked out of the window and waved.

Daniel hated the end of a first date. He never new how to act. Should he kiss Rouge, be available for a kiss, or should he just stay in the car.

The small house's door opened, and Robin stepped out.

"Mama is waiting for you," Daniel said.

Rouge shook his head. "With everything going on, he has kind of become the protector of the house." Opening the car door, "I had a really good time."

"Me too."

Rouge stepped out of the car and started walking toward the house.

Daniel noticed a rippling in the dark night, like a stone hurled into a pond. Someone or something concealed itself.

Following the ripples back to the tree line, he sought out the source.

Suddenly, the Dwayyo roared out of the woods and charged the house.

Daniel flung open the car door, and leapt out.

With a wave of his hand, he pushed Rouge up to the door.

"Get in!" he shouted.

Smoke filled his words.

The door slammed shut.

Flames spewed from his nostrils and mouth.

The Dwayyo slid in the grass.

It reared up, and snarled, gnashing his teeth.

Daniel sneered back.

His blood boiled.

He felt more powerful than he had ever felt before.

The beast's eyes widened.

Daniel blew fire at the dwayyo.

The heat scorched the air.

The light faded into deep shadow.

The Dwayyo howled in pain and ran for the forest.

Daniel calmed himself. The shadows lightened. He heard Nathan and Robin chanting in the house. Rouge stood at the window, his mouth gaping.

Chapter 15

Where did you go?

Daniel didn't sleep well. He knew Rouge saw him scare off the Dwayyo, and wasn't sure what to tell him when he inevitably asked about it. As the sky reddened with the morning sun, he dozed off.

A couple hours later, he woke up from the sun stinging his skin. He sighed. He shouldn't have fallen asleep with the drapes open. He should have known the heat would wake him up.

Giving up on sleeping, he walked into the kitchen to brew some coffee. Focus was more important than lounging about.

As the coffee brewed, he sat in meditation. He heightened his perceptions just like Castle taught him. He also listened for Oban's voice in the air. He missed him so much.

Harlow rustled in the other room.

Daniel shortened his meditations. He hopped up and headed for the kitchen. Pouring two cups of coffee, he listened to the room. Something was off. The light falling through the windows was too bright. He couldn't really focus his eyes well.

"Morning sunshine," Harlow bounded into the kitchen. "Where did you go last night?"

"I had a date last night with Rouge. We went out to Mortal Trust/Faerie Dust in Baltimore."

Harlow wilted. "I bet the harbor was beautiful in the moonlight."

"You know," Daniel sipped his coffee, "I didn't really notice. You know how long its been since I've been on a date. I was so nervous for the first half of the night."

"Then," Harlow picked up his coffee, "I suppose, it got better?"

Daniel thought about what to say next. He wanted to tell Harlow that he fought off the Dwayyo for the second time, but that would bring up too many questions.

"Yeah, it got better."

They prepared and ate a simple breakfast: a couple eggs, a few slices of bacon, and toast.

Daniel felt his pocket mirror calling to him. He walked into the living room, and picked it up off the coffee table.

Opening it, he saw Rouge smiling back.

"Hey girl," Daniel smiled. *Well, at least he wasn't afraid to talk to me.*

Rouge nodded, "Nathan wants me to help him finish warding the house, so I have to be quick. Can we meet this afternoon at The Cat Sith's Yarn, about three?"

"Sure."

Daniel arrived at the Cat Sith's Yarn a little early. It was a delightful Fae Pub down by the river.

He walked in, and picked a table by the window on the riverside. He ordered a strawberry melomel and watched the cat sith chasing each other around.

Rouge showed up a little while later.

Daniel rose up and gave him a hug, and led him back to the table.

After ordering a mulled cider, Rouge waited for the waiter to leave the table.

"I just wanted to say," Rouge said quietly, "Thank you for saving me yesterday. That was some real Gene Simmons shit. How'd you do it?"

Daniel bit his lip and waited for Rouge to sip his drink. "I told you I was learning how to weave illusions. We were just lucky the beast fell for it."

Rouge blinked a couple times. "Really? You fooled me too."

"Well," Daniel forced the lie, "If I am going to be responsible for the stagecraft at Wand and Weaver, then I need to be able to make it convincing."

"I suppose," Rouge sipped his cider.

"I mean, you know that Nathan wants me to organize an invocation of the Hobs to defend the people on the Wolf Moon."

"I know, he's been talking to Robin about it. He was afraid he would be offended."

"Was he?" Daniel asked.

"No, he said that Hobs are wild animals. They may resemble the Fae, but they are not."

Daniel was happy he was able to change the subject. He hoped Rouge would forget about it.

They talked for a while and finished their drinks.

After they paid the check, they got up and left the pub.

A dirty homeless person bumped into Daniel.

"Excuse you," Daniel said. Then he noticed... "Oban?"

The vagrant stumbled forward a few more steps.

"Castle," Daniel said, "Is that you?"

The vagrant turned slowly. "Daniel?"

Chapter 16

The Shadow of a Doubt

Tuesday, Robin decided to walk to Wand and Weaver. He was as happy as the others that Lady Oban showed up in town, but there was only so much he could take listening to people prattle on about it.

Besides he had his own issues. Didn't he always. At least this time wasn't because he pulled some stupid prank. He wasn't Alladin's genie, and he sure as hell was not Robin Williams.

He'd grinned and bore it for six hundred years. He just needed some time to refocus, a little time for himself. He knew it was selfish, but he had earned some non-jovial me time.

As he approached Wand and Weaver, he saw Jack standing in the parking lot.

Rolling his eyes, he debated his next move. Part of him wanted to attack. Give him the head of a Jack Ass. Maybe just turn around and go home...

That is exactly what Jack wanted. He knew he couldn't run from him forever, and frankly, didn't even have the energy to try.

"Morning, Ass," Robin waved.

Jack laughed, "Good afternoon, my good fellow. I hear your friend is home safe and sound."

"And if I find out that you had anything to do with that..."

"Calm down," Jack put his hands up, "I had nothing to do with that. I mean, don't think I haven't thought about recruiting your secret keeper for the Queen. He really loves nature, but I'm sure you already know that."

Robin forced a smile, "What do you want, Cú na Banríona?"

"Ouch," Jack brushed imaginary dirt off his shoulders. "Your pronunciation isn't what it used to be, but I suppose you are a little out of practice."

"What do you want?" Robin looked through him. He was so tired of the flea.

"I was just wondering," Jack said in a calm, calculating, smooth tone, "How long do you and your pet think you will be able to blackmail the Queen?

"Just long enough to prove I am a value to the Seelie Court out here."

Jack pursed his lips, "And all of the turmoil out here doesn't bother you?"

Robin cocked his head and smirked.

"Oberon misses you." Jack said, like he was talking to a runaway child about their puppy.

"And he would never let anything happen to me."

"O, he wouldn't," Jack raised an eyebrow, and walked toward the tree line.

Nathan brought Oban a hot tea, and sat it on the table in front of her. He hadn't let her out of his sight since she showed up Sunday in town.

She didn't remember a thing. She was at Wand and Weaver, then she was in town. She wouldn't go to the doctor, wouldn't talk to the authorities, wouldn't   take the day off.

It just wasn't right. She did her drag perfectly. Not a flaw in her makeup.

"Could you stop that?" She asked.

"Was I staring again?"

Oban nodded. "I love that you were so concerned about me, but you have to understand. I wasn't missing to me."

"Doesn't the lost time bother you?" Nathan asked.

"Yes and no," Oban shrugged. "It is a mystery. I am a secret keeper. It fascinates me more than it bothers me. It has been a long time since I was a mystery to myself."

Nathan allowed his shoulders to relax. "I suppose I can see that."

"What bothers me more than anything, is that you are keeping something from me. What's going on between you and Emrys? You are worrying so much about it that I can hardly concentrate."

Nathan looked around to make sure they were alone. "Cyn said some horrible things about me and Emrys. She thinks that we, or at least that I am living in a fantasy."

"Why?" Oban swiveled away from the mirror. "Do you think they used to be friends, or more?"

"Honestly, I can't imagine Cyn being with anyone."

"Why would..." Oban trailed off, "I mean Cyn... Maybe..." Oban looked off into the distance, opening and closing her mouth a couple times as if something was on the tip of her tongue. She just couldn't bring herself to say it.

Harlow plopped down in one of the bar stools.

"Cosmo," She said to Robin, "Pretty please with whip cream, sugar, and a cherry on top."

Robin blinked at her, "I refuse to put any of that shit on a Cosmo. I don't give a damn how girly you want it to be." He winked at her.

"Stupid fairy," she slapped at him. "I wanna sulk dammit. Don't make me laugh."

"How about a giggle?" Robin slid the Cosmo in front of her. "Would you like a straw for that?"

Harlow sighed and snatched the drink away from him. "Stop that."

The horns and marching band announced the start of Madonna and Justin Timberlake's 4 Minutes.

"Oh," Robin dropped his head like a naughty child, "Your Valentine and his Valentino are on. You should have asked for something harder."

"Like a hammer?" Harlow half-smiled.

"Like whisky you trashy ho."

"Flattery will get you no where old man," Harlow said, "I'm not into archeology."

Robin laughed. "You know, there isn't anything real there. I've played with 'love-in-idleness.' I can see the difference between love, lust, and infatuation. That is the latter."

Harlow winced and wanted to cry, but swallowed her tears with a sip of Cosmo. "You think you could get me a couple flowers."

"Never!" Robin shook his head.

Someone grabbed Harlow's arm.

She turned around.

Lady Oban stood there. Eyes wide and wild, lips quivering.

"Something..." Oban said holding onto Harlow for dear life. "Something is wrong with me."

"What is it?" Harlow asked.

"There is a shadow," Oban acted like each word hurt, "A shadow in my mind. It eclipses... I can't get past it. It is growing. Oh, God, I can feel it growing."

Chapter 17

Show Me the Way

The audience applauded their rendition of 4 Minutes.

Marley and Rouge exited to stage left, and scurried back to the makeup room to make sure they hadn't melted.

Relief flooded her sigh. Marley collapsed in the chair in front of her mirror, and examined herself closely. "I know I am a dancer, but that pushed it a bit."

"O Danny boy," Rouge giggled, "You push yourself too hard. We aren't in New York, Evonium, or Ker-Ys. These people won't know if you take it easy."

"I've dreamed of performing in Ker-Ys, and sweetie," Marley looked at Rouge, "I would know if I didn't do my best. That is worse than a bad review."

"Perfectionist."

"Slacker"

They laughed.

Marley carefully examined her forehead for runny makeup. "It's no ones fault they were born in a small town. They deserve a great show too."

"It is if they choose to live here," Rouge stuck his tongue out.

"So what's your excuse?" Marley raised a well painted eyebrow.

"Now, now." Rouge wagged her finger. "I was born here. So let's not judge."

Marley twisted side to side in her chair, "I suppose we should head back out."

"Eh," Rouge said, "Nathan will sound last call soon. We can head out for close. Right now, just put your feet up and relax."

Marley wanted to argue, but it felt so good to be sitting down she just couldn't. She leaned back in her chair and let her muscles relax.

"How is Nathan taking everything?" Marley asked.

"What do you mean?"

"The Dwayyo attacking twice outside his house. Castle's return. The success of the Fetehouse. His best friend dating me."

"Nathan is Nathan." Rouge said. "He would worry no matter what happened. I am not sure if these stresses are good or bad for him. At least he is worrying about real things, and it's not all in his head."

"I think that is why we get along so well," Marley said, "I am a worrier too."

"O, Daniel, why would someone like you worry about anything? You are more than a match for anything."

"What do you mean by that?" Marley sat up.

"You know exactly what I am talking about. You may not want to know what I mean, but you do."

Marley's heart pounded.

She felt the heat rushing through her chest and arms. Instinctively, she wanted to attack.

"I'm not sure what you are talking about." Marley said, "What do you mean?"

Rouge smiled at her. "Do you want me to say it? There are only two reasons you would be so worried about a Ryukishi coming to town. Only one reason explains your eyes when you get angry."

"Like now." Marley's voice rumbled.

"Yes, and it's not a good look on you, by the way."

Marley reached into her pocket and ran her thumb across the charm. "Then, shouldn't you be careful. If I am what you think I am..."

"You're what," Rouge stepped closer. "Dangerous? If you weren't a good person, you would have let the Dwayyo get me."

Marley didn't feel like Marley anymore. He didn't feel like Daniel either. Rage and hunger boiled under his skin.

The room looked different. Currents of energy flowed in, through, and around everything like a cascade of light from a rock concert.

He wanted to kill Rouge. Rip the life from his body.

Anger and euphoria danced through his veins.

"Don't worry," he heard Rouge say, "I won't tell anyone."

The voice was distant, like a radio in another room.

"Marley?"

Whose voice was that? It was familiar. Silky, seductive.

"Marley, your scales are showing. Breath dear."

He took in a deep breath. The air tasted so sweet, rich, and luxurious. Narcotic.

"There you go child. Just breath. It will all be alright."

Haze enveloped his sight. His muscle relaxed. Slipping into the chair, his eyes tried to focus. He saw Cyn taking the steps up to the stage.

Cyn took the darkened stage. The drum and bass of Elis' Show me the Way pounded through the speakers. The guitar crunched, the lights flared to life.

Lip syncing, Cyn danced to the beat. Her movements were slow as if dancing in water. Light flashed above her; she smiled. Folding her hands over her heart, she looked right at Mira in the crowd.

She chose the song on purpose. It was a confessional. She still hadn't found the confidence to tell Mira the whole truth, but the spell and potion were working, and soon there would be no turning back.

A luminous specter of Cyn as a priestess stepped off to her left. Cyn rolled her hips seductively, An angelic phantom stepped off to her right.

The three turned their back to the audience.

The priestess spun and fell to her knees.

Cyn twirled around opening her arms to embrace the room.

Golden light sparked from the angel as it leapt into the air.

The sparks rushed into ribbons from the angel to the priestess, to Cyn and back again.

In a blink, there were three of each on the stage, then only three.

The spell only had one chance to work, and by the end of the week, the truth would be moot.

Cyn turned to the angel pleading, and danced around her. Fog flooded the stage, through which a road emerged moving in front of her.

She smiled at Mira, and continued the performance. She could feel Mira like her own skin. The connection was strong. By the end of the week, the enchantment would snap and she would be free.

Mira looked away.

Cyn felt cold as the song ended.

The audience applauded.

Something stirred within her. She knew she found the answer within her.

She rushed off the stage, and outside into the brisk night air. Steam rose off her body.

The moon light echoed through her. Her skin tightened. The magic banded around her arms, legs, and chest.

She could hear the howling in the distance. The Dwayyo was on the hunt... Or was it?

Why hadn't it killed anyone other than Lauren Travers? It had so many opportunities. Did it live on fear? Maybe she was associated with someone she shouldn't have been.

Cyn thought about stories Ash had told her about creatures that lived on fear just like she lived off desire. They were ancient, and nearly impossible to kill.

The magic constricted again. The spell wasn't ready, she couldn't let the power overwhelm her.

Her skin burned like wax too close to a flame.

It didn't show. Not yet. Once the last name was spoken, and potion was ready, she knew the pain would be unbearable. That was for later. These were the early stages. It would only get worse.

The cool air soothed her skin.

Light flashed from her body as the magic released.

Inhaling, Cyn looked around to make sure no one saw her. She wished she had made it to the tree line, but the parking lot was empty.

As Cyn walked back in, the clientele exited. She wondered how long she was outside. She missed last call, so it had to be close to an hour. It didn't feel like an hour.

She cursed under her breath.

Robin was wiping down the bar, and Marley was sweeping up. She was happy to see Marley pulled it back together.

Cyn's emotions ran wild. She could see a lot of herself in Marley. She had her secrets too, and she didn't know how to hold it all in yet.

She knew Marley might kill her if she knew Cyn had figured her out. She didn't think Marley had it in her. Well, Marley might, but Daniel didn't. Personas don't often take a life of their own.

Mira was over by the stage with Lady Oban, Harlow, and Rouge.

"So, did you make your mind up?" Rouge asked Mira.

"I am going to tell Emrys that I love him," Mira said, "Damn Cyn, and whatever she thinks about the two of us. She wouldn't know love if Cupid shot her in the chest. Love is sacrifice. And Cyn doesn't know a thing about sacrifice."

Cyn wanted to slap Mira so hard Nathan fell out.

She pulled it all in, and thundered toward the door, slamming into Robin.

"Watch it!" Robin steadied himself. "What's the matter with you?"

Cyn seethed, and narrowed her eyes, "Your friend, Mira Nathan Clueless Kell is about to make a big mistake, and she doesn't even know."

"What are you talking about?"

"You can only tempt a wolf for so long before it snaps its chain and gets you."

Chapter 18

Courage of the Knife

Nathan had a rough weekend. He called Emrys several times, but he didn't answer. Why didn't he answer?

He thought about all the things that Cyn said about Emrys, and their relationship, and wondered if it had been a fantasy, nothing more than a dream.

Emrys was so sweet, kind, and romantic. Everything Nathan wanted in a relationship, but no one could be that perfect. He had to have some flaws, but Nathan was damned if he could remember any. If a person is flawless, they can't be real, can they?

Cyn might be right. Nathan hated the very thought of that. More than likely, with all of the chaos and upheaval in his life, he probably just overlooked anything that could be a problem or issue.

That made sense, didn't it. He needed Emrys to be an oasis in the stress, and... that made Cyn right.

Nathan knew he had to let it go. If Emrys hadn't done anything wrong, how could he hold that against him. It was the stupidest thought he'd ever had.

You can't be upset with someone for not upsetting you. It was simple. He let Cyn get into his mind. That just couldn't be allowed.

There was nothing wrong with having a good time. Even if it was nothing more than a fantasy.

Wait, Nathan thought, *Emrys has disappointed me. He's not answering my call. He's not always there when I need him. That hardly makes him a fantasy or a dream.*

That was all it took for Nathan to cheer up. If he could see a flaw and still love him than it couldn't be a simple infatuation.

Love is only love when it survives impact with reality.

Tuesday morning, he bounded out of his bedroom, and into the kitchen. He tapped a small crystal ball on the counter, the broadview sparkled to life.

The morning news was on. After he watched the weather report, cool with clear skies, he walked over to the refrigerator to make breakfast.

Robin and Rouge were still in bed, but he knew the smell of bacon would wake them up. So he put enough in the pan for the three of them.

Behind the sizzle of the bacon, he heard Chloe Riley's trained and cultured voice say, "Herald of Philadelphia, Paul Kincaid ended his visit to Seton County this morning with a prayer service at the public altar to Consus in the heart of Schleyfield."

Nathan almost fell down. His eyes locked with the visage of the steely faced, gray haired man in the image.

"May Consus forgive us for our trespasses which caused him to weaken our ward of protection," the Herald said, "Allowing the Dwayyo to return to haunt our nights and terrorize our people. And may the giants forgive Nathan Kell for his heresy, for which the county is now being punished."

Nathan's blood froze.

He couldn't have heard what he just heard. That didn't just happen.

"We tried to contact Mr Kell for a response," Chloe said, "But he does not have a public glass. We will continue to follow this story as we look into the Herald's accusations."

"Your bacon is burning," Robin said behind him.

Nathan flipped the bacon and just watched the grease sputter in the pan.

"You know for a fact he is full of shit," Robin said as he sat down.

"Y... yeah," Nathan forced the words. He didn't want to breathe much less talk, "But the county doesn't know that."

"Then tell them."

"You expect people to take the word of a proclaimed heretic over that of a Herald of the Covenant?"

"Why not?" Robin slapped his palms on the table. "He is not the Herald of... uh, which Herald is over this area?"

Nathan took the bacon out of the frying pan, and cracked in a couple eggs. "It doesn't matter. True or not, it's my fault now. The news said so."

"You are taking this all too seriously. Only one person has been killed, and they were a deannaigh Si dealer. No loss to the community there. Yes, people are scared, but it's not that bad."

"You really don't understand our world do you?"

"Not the point." Robin said, "This is a perception issue. Talk to Oban. It's nothing more than tricks of light and shadow. We can work with this."

"How?" Nathan flipped the eggs hard, breaking the yolks. "He might as well have sewn a scarlet A on my chest."

"Melodrama much? How much of our clientele even care what another city's Herald has to say."

Nathan hoped Robin was right.

Cyn had a rough weekend. A lot of questions about why Nathan was still alive. She was sick of it all. She spent most of her time in the forest avoiding the problem.

She knew the spell and potion was working, or someone would be dead.

After she heard what the Herald said on Tuesday, she went into Wand and Weaver early.

The Channel Alaunus news van was set up in the parking lot, and Chloe and her sphero operator were set up by the door to ambush Nathan.

Cyn knew she would probably regret it, but she called on the shadows to shatter the recording crystal in the operators hand.

"What the hell are you doing here?" She walked up on Chloe and looked down on her. "This is a happy place, and you are a carrier of lies."

Chloe puffed herself up, "And just who are you?"

"Me?" Cyn tossed her hair back. "I am someone who knows your Herald very well, and knows that he is a liar, a criminal, and a blasphemer."

With a wave of her hand, Cyn brushed them away from the door toward the van.

"If I were you," Cyn pulled the warmth of the sunlight from the air, "I would retract your lies, and look into Paul's life, and associations."

"What do you mean by that?" Chloe asked.

"Look into the Gram Society."

"The what?" Realization dawned on her face. "Are you insinuating..."

"All I said is that you might want to look into the Gram Society." Cyn blanked her face. "I think you will find a good story that the whole commonwealth might be interested in. Maybe even the whole Sith Thyrsa."

Cyn could see the wheels rolling in her mind.

Chloe whispered something to her sphero operator, then the two of them got into the van and drove away.

Filled with vindictive glee, Cyn reveled in the controversy she just set into motion. The Herald would be disgraced, and at least that should clear Nathan's good name.

The Gram Society were secretive, so she might have to pepper a few more hints before the story broke, but it would be done.

Cyn waited for about thirty minutes for Nathan, Robin and Rouge to show up.

Nathan was so down, Cyn's blood burned.

She wanted to comfort Nathan, but that was not in her nature.

"Are you upset about about that Herald thing?" Cyn asked.

"Yes," Nathan said, "I am surprised reporters weren't camping out."

"I took care of it. That should clear up soon."

"Oh, like it's that easy." Nathan fought back tears, "Do you have any idea what I lost when he kicked me out of the priesthood? What the stakes were for me having to come back here? I have disgraced my family. You just don't get it. You've never given up anything, have you?"

Cyn looked at Nathan with a cold glare that could make it snow, "How have you managed to live this long? You feel everything, every little fucking thing! If words can cut you, then you are going to bleed to death. This is Paulie's problem, not yours! You should pity him. Instead, you are letting him control you."

Nathan was so happy people showed up for the night. Several pulled him aside and told him that they didn't believe a word of what the Herald said.

He called Emrys several times but no answer.

Nathan started to worry. What was going on? Was this how Emrys broke up with people. He hoped that wasn't the case. That was too much for him to bear.

After Wand and Weaver closed, he decided to go to Emrys' house. Nathan arranged for Robin and Rouge to get a ride home with Daniel.

Now for the real challenge. He didn't know exactly where Emrys lived. He knew he had a place out in Mulberry Hills, so he drove out that way hoping to make a plan along the way.

He hoped he would be able to see something that would let him know which house was Emrys'. He needed to see him, needed to be in those arms. He had to know why he was incommunicado.

Maybe he was out of town.

As he passed the Mulberry Hills sign, he wondered if he was making a mistake. Maybe one of the neighbors would call the authorities on the strange man in the car driving around.

In the light of the street lamps ahead, he saw someone walking. Someone familiar.

It was Cyn.

How did she get from Wand and Weaver to Mulbery Hills so fast?

Nathan parked his car on the side of the road, and watched Cyn walk for a moment. He had to know what was going on. Were Cyn and Emrys dating? Is that why Cyn was trying to scare him off?

He slipped out of the car, and followed her.

She pulled a hip flask out of her pocket, and took a swig.

Nathan hid behind a bush as she crossed the lane in front of him. Energy swelled in the air. Constricting, suffocating, power.

Shadows dripped off Cyn like water. Her hair blackened, straightened, and shortened, but not too short. Her eyes turned blue.

Nathan gasped.

Emrys turned toward him, "What have you done?" Pain crackled, as the whites of his eyes turned black.

"How?" Nathan said.

"Do you have any idea what you've done? You couldn't know."

"What! That you have been lying to me?"

"I had to!" Emrys sobbed, wincing with pain. "You've ruined everything."

"I did? I wasn't the one fucking with your mind."

"I wasn't. I was trying to warn you."

"That you are a monster?"

"Yes!" Emrys collapsed and howled in agony. "I tried to tell you, but..."

"But what? You were having too much fun with your little game?"

"This is not a game," Emrys screamed like his bones were shattering.

"Then what the fuck was it?"

"I loved you." The shadow under Emrys grew. "Now... I can never be with you!" His tone deadened. "You might want to run."

"Or you'll hurt me more?"

"Can't you understand," Emrys' eyes gleamed like an eclipse. "It is too dangerous for you to be here. I am too dangerous."

Shadowy wings grew from his back, and he jumped into the air. He looked down on Nathan and flew up. Calling down to him, "I gave up everything for you. I broke my word, repressed my nature, and still you couldn't trust me enough. Love without trust is dead!"

Chapter 19

Angry Shadows

Nathan stood in the cold watching Emrys fly away. His last words cut through Nathan's heart. What did he mean? Love without trust is dead. None of it made sense to him. Had he betrayed his betrayer?

He walked back to his car for what felt like an hour. He searched his memory, hoping he would be able to figure out what went wrong with this life. Something must have happened. He had followed one dream to a dead end, and now, he felt like two other dreams died tonight.

Leaning against his car, he let himself cry. He was shocked his mother hadn't called him yet. Maybe she wouldn't. Maybe this was it. He was finally revealed to the world as the failure he was. His sister hadn't called either. He'd never felt so alone.

Nathan opened the door, and collapsed into his seat. As he closed the door, he winced at the sound of the door closing. What did Emrys mean by concealing his nature? He felt like a selfish fool for yelling at Cyn.

I deserve to be alone. He thought.

He started the car, and drove home.

The lights were off at the house. He turned off the engine and sat in the car for a moment. Getting out, he walked up to the door, unlocked it, and pushed his way in.

Robin snored from the couch, and Rouge from his room.

Nathan walked into his own room, and sat on the bed. Nothing felt right anymore. The decor even looked grayer. He took off his shoes and laid them on the floor so he wouldn't wake the others up. He slipped under the covers.

Laying there, he stared at the ceiling until he fell asleep.

The next day, he went into work and didn't even bother getting into makeup. He spent most of his time in his office.

Cyn didn't show up. Nathan didn't expect him to. He called Emrys a couple times, and his mirror got so cold. Emrys wasn't going to talk to him again. He knew that.

Emrys was gone. Cyn was gone.

Daniel did his best to reassign Cyn's numbers to the other queens, and had to come up with a few others.

People showed up for the night, but business was down.

Paul won. If turnout stayed this low, he would have a hard time paying the bills. He had a couple months before he had to start worrying about that too much.

Nathan wondered how much Cyn had to do with propping up business. Maybe he didn't know how much they relied on him. Perhaps they would be lost without him.

Why couldn't Cyn just tell him the truth from the start? What had Emrys given up? Who did he break his word to? What was he?

He wasn't a Ryukishi. His wings were made of shadows, not skin. He wasn't an Erythrai. They don't have black on black eyes. He wasn't a fae. He didn't show any of the signs, and besides, Robin would have known.

He said I didn't trust him enough, he didn't trust me with anything. Secrets are harmful. They don't benefit anyone. They hurt the one who harbors them and the one they are kept from.

The week lingered on.

Nathan was present through it all, but nothing really earned too much of his attention. Daniel had some ideas about how to drum up business. Robin introduced some new drink specials. Nathan just left it all to them.

He kept to himself. He questioned everything. He had always trusted his own sense of right and wrong. He trusted his conscience, but now he didn't know if he could trust it anymore. He didn't know if his conscience was hindering or helping him.

If Cyn and Emrys were the same person, and he couldn't see it, how could he trust any of his thoughts, feelings, or impressions anymore.

He showed up everyday at Wand and Weaver. Everyday, he hoped he would get back into the groove, and to get back to work, but really wanted to be alone.

Several times, he tried different things to get himself back to some semblance of normal. Nothing worked. He just kept to himself in the office while the Fetehouse was open, bouncing between anger and depression.

Rouge told him that if he didn't get it together he was going to lose Wand and Weaver. He knew that. He just had no clue how to make it better.

Robin watched Nathan fall apart. Every time he or Rouge tried to intervene, he just brushed them off. Robin didn't know what to do. He knew it had to be big. Something Nathan couldn't ignore.

He couldn't get over how much Nathan reminded him of Oberon. He was a light free spirit who too often tarred his own wings with guilt and self-doubt. Granted, he had Titania and her children to pull him down.

Every time Oberon was in a funk, like that, he pulled a prank. That's how he ended up involved with the bard all those years ago.

A prank wouldn't work this time around. Robin knew Nathan didn't respond well to pranks. It would simply backfire.

It took him a couple weeks to formulate a plan, but once he had it he set his mind.

That Thursday, he rode into Wand and Weaver with Nathan and Rouge.

When Nathan parked the car, Robin said, "So, are you getting into drag today?"

Nathan stepped out of the car.

Robin hopped out of the car on the same side. "I mean, it's been a few weeks since sultry and scary flew the coup. Why mourn the loss of someone who lost themselves?"

Nathan walked toward the door.

"That's neither a yes nor a no," Robin said. "You are always talking to me about responsibility. I really don't see the point of it."

Nathan stopped.

"I mean, this is a fun sandbox."

He watched Nathan's muscles tense, and knew it was close.

"Isn't this the time to get serious? I mean, I know the cliche, but to give up everything for love feels like a raw deal to me. I mean, I would never pay a cent for undelivered goods."

Nathan sneered at Robin.

"Maybe you would work on a cover of Two out of Three Ain't Bad, after all the only thing you got was want and need. There was no love."

"What the fuck do you know about love?" Nathan spun around and snarled. "You playful little fairy who always has a smile and a trick up your sleeve. Who the hell do you think you of all creatures are to talk to me like that! Play your part- flitter around and trick people out of their money, and keep your nose out of my business."

"If that's what you want."

Robin smiled as Nathan went into Wand and Weaver. He hoped he had focused all Nathan's anger at Cyn, Emrys, and the situation at himself. He knew it was a start, but if he could handle being the focus of Titania's anger, Nathan would be easy.

Lady Oban was surprised to see Nathan at his makeup mirror that Thursday. She heard him curse Robin under his breath several times, and thought better than to ask about it.

They had a decent crowd, but nothing compared to what it had been.

Oban focused on her work, but kept seeing something out of the corner of her eye. She knew it wasn't something outside her mind. It was within.

After work, as she wiped Oban from his face, he saw the shadow again. This time it pressed on his mind.

"Are you alright?" Daniel asked.

"No." Castle picked himself up from the counter. He didn't even know he'd laid his head on the counter. "I need your help."

"Anything, hon," Daniel said.

"I need to borrow your strength tonight."

"For what?"

"Exposing a secret."

Daniel agreed without another question.

As soon as Castle felt like traveling, they got into Daniel's car, and drove to Castle's apartment.

In the apartment, Castle gathered up a number of candles, and set them up in a half circle in front of the couch.

"I hope you have been keeping up with your daily practice." Castle said as he lit the candles. "I need to know what happened to me. Something is wrong with me."

"I am glad you finally came around." Daniel said.

Castle sat down in the middle of the semicircle. "When you are ready, turn off the lights. I need you to focus on the light, and no matter what happens, don't let the light go out."

Daniel nodded.

"I am going to focus on the shadows until the secret is revealed." Castle relaxed his muscles and centered his mind.

He tried to extend his mind between the candles. There was a wall. He noticed when Daniel turned off the room's lights, but didn't feel the change in luminance.

Castle centered himself again. He pushed at the corners of his mind. Something struggled. It felt like a bubble in the middle of his mind. A foreign body that he couldn't relate to at all.

He imagined a form for it. A foggy cloud that roughly fit the contours of the bubble. It fought him. He constricted the image, pretending it was an iron maiden trapping the shadow.

Taking a deep breath in, Castle took hold of the iron maiden. He projected it into the light of the candles.

A black shadow rushed out of him and pressed against the light.

Brick by brick, Castle built a wall in his mind. As he inserted the last brick, he let go of the tether.

The shadow fled from the circle.

Castle looked up at Daniel.

"I remember now."

Chapter 20

Truth and Warning

Nathan sat in his office. He glanced over the Friday schedule. He had no numbers on the list, so he decided not to get dolled up.

A knock on the door.

"Come in," He said without looking up.

Lady Oban entered dressed like a New Orleans Fortune Teller. "I really need to talk to you."

"Have a seat," Nathan looked up from his papers.

"Daniel told me not to tell you, but I think you have to know." Oban fidgeted in her seat. "You know I couldn't remember what happened to me when I lost time." She steadied herself. "I now know, but please don't interrupt me until I am done."

"Ok," Nathan leaned back in his chair.

Oban took a deep breath. "The night I disappeared, I was with Cyn. I had discovered her secret, and wanted to tell her about it. I told her that she had to tell you, or I would."

"I know that Cyn is Emrys." Nathan winced.

"That's not it." Oban said. "Cyn is a cambion."

"A what?"

"The offspring of an incubus or succubus and a human."

"That..." Nathan thought about his intoxicating presence, and his natural allure. "That makes sense."

"He was hired by the Herald of Philadelphia to disgrace and kill you."

Nathan's heart broke, "So it was all a lie, then."

Oban stuttered for a moment, "No. He couldn't do it. After I confronted him, he trapped me in this shadow web. I couldn't move. I thought he was going to kill me. He broke down, and I saw the real him. He loves you. He kept cursing a drink and a dance."

Nathan remembered Wand and Weaver's opening night. The dances they shared.

"He was supposed to poison you that night. He was so scared how you would react if you knew."

Shame beat Nathan in the gut.

"He also said," Oban straightened her back, "The Herald's office told him to blame the Dwayyo attacks on the spreading heresy in the county."

"Any when Emrys didn't do it, Paul did." Nathan felt his confidence melting.

"He didn't know what to do with me," Oban continued, "So he used his powers to make me forget. But it made me forget everything. So I wandered around until Daniel found me."

Nathan didn't know what to say. He felt like he betrayed everyone. He thought about what the giants said. Fritha never directly answered the question about the Dwayyo.

"Thank you, Oban," Nathan said. "You did the right thing."

After Oban left his office, Nathan debated what was the right thing for him to do. If he could find Emrys, he could ask if the Dwayyo was his fault. If he couldn't find Emrys or if it was his fault, *Maybe I should just let the Dwayyo have me so this will all be over.*

Nathan woke up Saturday feeling like he hadn't slept a minute. He heard Robin and Rouge joking around in the kitchen. He missed that jovial spirit. He wanted so much to join them, but everything weighed him down. He felt like he did when he was a kid and broke his leg. He could hear the kids playing in the neighborhood, but couldn't join them.

He pulled out a candle and his gazing crystal.

Balling up all his emotions into a knot in his chest, he positioned his hand in line with the crystal and the flame. He pushed the knot down his arm. It tugged at his chest, so he pressed harder.

He felt the strands of feeling extrude from his fingertips, wrapping like silk around the crystal. He anchored in the flame.

Tethered to the ritual he allowed his yearning for Emrys to echo through the room.

Light flickered in the crystal.

Nathan felt Emrys like he was in the room. He was so close. He searched the crystal for any sign of him.

Nothing.

He allowed himself to want it more.

Emrys knew he was looking.

Nathan could feel his longing, and his anger.

Binding their pain together, Nathan tried to follow the strands to a point, a place, a region. Any hint where he could find Emrys.

He flooded his urgency and desperation through the connection. He felt Emrys wilt under it.

"Please let me find you," Nathan whispered.

Emrys pulled away.

Nathan tried to hold the connection. They needed to talk so bad.

Nothing.

The chain broke. He still had no idea where Emrys was.

Daniel felt something strange in the air all day Saturday. Several times he felt like someone walked over his grave.

The queens were somber at Wand and Weaver.

Nathan stayed in his office all day, which Daniel was getting used to. There had to be something he could do to help Nathan out of his funk.

Harlow walked around like her heart was broken.

Robin was jumpy.

Rouge was done with everything.

Castle was the only one who acted like he was in a good mood. As he transformed into Lady Oban he looked like a Gaultier Sun Goddess.

Daniel wanted to contrast with her, so he put on his best Rick Owens and makeup to match. Marley loved the dark look.

That night at Wand and Weaver was slow. The regulars showed up, but not a lot of other people.

Marley performed like they had a packed house. She knew if they kept the quality up, the people would come back.

After close, she washed Marley off, and put on his Rick Owens menswear. Castle wanted him to come out to celebrate his memories triumphant return.

Daniel didn't feel like celebrating. He just wanted to go home. The odd feelings didn't go away. If something was about to go down, he thought it would be better if he were alone.

He drove home well under the speed limit. The closer he got to his apartment, the stronger the feeling became. It didn't feel like a dragon, a ryukishi, or an erythrai. It was similar. It could be someone trying to mask their presence.

As he pulled into the parking lot, a strange man in a black overcoat exited his building.

The stranger stopped on the sidewalk. He turned toward Daniel and bowed his head. Flipping his coat off his back, large black leather wings rose into the sky. With a wave of his hand, the stranger leapt into the night and flew away.

Daniel kept his eye on the sky as he made his way into the building.

A black envelope was tied to his door knob with a white ribbon.

He didn't want to open it. He didn't want to know what it said.

Reaching for the envelope, he felt the air for any hint of magic that would indicate a trap. He snatched the envelope from the ribbon and opened it.

Written on the parchment was:

Daniel,

The Redd Bishop has the Queen in check, prepare the Rooks.

Black Night

He blinked twice. The only words that made sense to him were his name and Redd Bishop. They were a media company. What was this about?

Chapter 21

Into the Furnace

Nathan slept in Sunday morning. He wanted to go in to the shrine today. He needed guidance. Forgetting to set an alarm was not part of the plan.

He dressed and fixed a little brunch. Robin and Rouge tried to strike up conversations with him, but he just wasn't in the mood.

Once he made it to the shrine, all of his guilt and worry surfaced. He stood outside for a long time, debating whether he should force himself to go in.

He walked around the outside. Prayers fell like leadened rain from his lips. His heart wasn't in it. He wanted his heart to be in it.

His faith was light, and jangled like broken glass. He was a pilgrim on his way to avalon who went over the hill and found himself in a different world. The constellations were unfamiliar. He lost the north star.

He entered the shrine. The air was thick with the morning's incense. He was alone amid the statues and the stained glass.

In the niche of the way, he knelt before the altar. He lit a candle and opened himself to the divine mystery.

"In the name of all that is holy, and in concert with the holy ones who have gone before, please hear me. Father always said that we must empty ourselves of all the old to make way for the new. I am so empty."

Nathan leaned on the kneeler. "I've lost everything. My name, my love, my dreams. All gone. All I have left is my life and my friends."

He sniffled, wanting to cry. "What am I suppose to do? If Wand and Weaver doesn't work, I will have nothing left. This has to work. I cannot see a way through this. I've done all I know how to do. I've given everything. What do you want?"

His eyes burned from the absence of tears, "What further sacrifices can I make? Help me. Oh, please help me."

Nathan's breathing broke into sobs, but he still couldn't cry. He wanted his tears to wash away his pain.

Nothing happened.

He didn't expect the heavens to open up and the answer to come down on stone tablets, but he hoped he would feel something. He didn't know if his pain was holding him back from finding any release.

His future felt so dark. It constricted him. He needed to break out. He needed to do something dramatic.

Nathan drove out to the Catoctan Furnace. He decided to offer himself up to the Dwayyo. He had always heard that the beast was connected to Wolf Rock, so it would have to pass by that way on its way to Schleyfield. He knew he would either defeat the Dwayyo, or it would kill him. If he was the reason it came, his death would dispel it. If not, it would at least be over.

The sun was low in the sky, and it would be dark soon. He walked around the old stone buildings for a while. This place was special to him. He met Robin in the Catoctan woods. He spent a lot of time here.

He drew strength from this place. Cannonballs for the American Revolution were made here. He thought about that lust for freedom, and the courage to stand up to a mighty empire. He needed that strength to face what was to come.

He only saw one problem with the location. It was close to a wrecca community, and he didn't want to risk any of their lives.

Walking north, he followed the Catoctin Furnace Trail. He crossed Little Hunting Creek, then 15 on the pedestrian overpass.

Every step reminded him of his childhood. He knew these woods. It felt like home.

He stopped by the Visitor Center. He thought he heard footsteps.

Looking around, he strained his eyes to see if something was there. He couldn't see anything or anyone. He felt like he wasn't alone.

He continued on the path to the Catoctin Trail.

As he walked through the woods, he started thinking about Little Red Riding Hood and the Big Bad Wolf. He hoped he was the woodsman and not Red Riding Hood or Grandma.

Someone else was following or shadowing him. He could hear their footsteps just off the trail. He still couldn't see them. He looked, but nothing. It was impossible to tell what was tree and what was a person.

It was a person following him. The footfalls were too light to be the Dwayyo. He heard its footsteps outside his house. They were heavy. These were light.

After High Run, he took the path towards Cat Rock.

Whoever was following him along the path was still there. He wondered if it was Robin. It couldn't be. A fae wouldn't make a sound in the forest. That is why most people missed them.

The silver white stones of Cat Rock were off to his right. For a split second, he thought he saw someone standing in the clearing.

It couldn't have been whoever was following him. He could hear them snapping twigs on the other side of the path.

When he reached the fork in the trail, he debated whether he wanted to go North Northeast toward Chimney Rock, or North west toward the dam.

Something growled behind him. There was an energy in the air. The air crackled like lightening was about to strike.

Nathan turned around as slow as he could.

The beast stood in the middle of the trail. It loomed at least nine feet tall, and sniffed the air. It bore its teeth like a gray wolf warning an inferior to back off.

He stood his his ground.

The Dwayyo growled and snarled.

"I am here." Nathan said. "You've shown a lot of interest in me and my house. You want me. I am here."

The beast watched him. Moonlight gleamed on its teeth.

Nathan threw all his anger at the beast. It ignited as it left his hand and impacted in the center of its chest.

The creature slid back, growled and lunged at Nathan.

He jumped out of the way, and turned to face it.

Something rustled beyond the tree line, and a swarm of hornets, wasps, and yellowjackets attacked the Dwayyo.

The beast howled in pain and shock. It swatted at the swarm but couldn't kill enough of them. It ran off into the woods toward Bear Branch.

Nathan collapsed on the ground.

None of the insects remained in the air.

Where did they even come from? No hives should be that active in February.

The Dwayyo's howls of pain ripped through the cold night air.

"Did one of you do this?" Nathan called out to the heavens. "Why?" He screeched. "Nothing's changed. Nothing. I'm not even allowed to die?" He wiped the tears out of his eyes.

"I just wanted it to be over. One way or another, over. Why couldn't I at least have that."

He ran the encounter through his mind over and over again. He didn't even scratch the Dwayyo. He knocked it back on its heels, but he didn't even scratch it.

Nathan picked himself up.

He thought about walking back to his car, but he wanted to see at least one thing through. So he followed the steep trail over the ridge and down to Hunting Creek Lake.

Nathan was surprised the Dwayyo didn't return.

He sat on the small, grayed wood pier over the lake and waited for the sun to come up. The cool breeze over the blue black water chilled him, but he was glad he at least felt something.

He had exhausted all his ideas. What was left? He couldn't defeat the beast, and couldn't even offer his life to it.

Who sent the swarms? Someone protected him, but he didn't know who or why. He didn't deserve protection.

Someone walked on the boards behind him.

Nathan didn't turn.

An old fisherman, bundled up against the cold walked over to the other side of the small pier.

"It's a little cold to be fishing, don't you think?" Nathan asked.

"I like to test my line every day," the fisherman laughed. "Why are you out here so early? Don't you know, the Dwayyo has been seen around these parts."

Nathan smiled, *Yeah, just last night,* he thought. "I am the reason the Dwayyo is here. You probably saw it on the news."

"Oh, you mean what Paulie said?" The fisherman chuckled. "Don't you understand, the Dwayyo is a creature of rage and fear. You can only fight it if you starve it of rage and fear. Besides, I'm not convinced that everything is exactly what it appears to be."

"Then what is it?" Nathan asked.

"Tough."

Something in his tone was familiar.

Nathan looked over to thank the fisherman, but he was gone.

Standing up, he looked around for the old man. He was alone. While he didn't understand what just happened, he started thinking up a plan.

Chapter 22

Give My Heart

Nathan gathered the queens as soon as he got back home. Together, they filtered around town hanging fliers in drag, and drumming up excitement for the coming week.

He was so tired when he got home. He just collapsed in bed, and slept like a rock until the alarm went off.

After everything, he had no where to go but up. Wand and Weaver was young. He couldn't give up on it.

He, Robin, and Rouge packed into the car, and headed in.

His blood froze as they pulled into the Wand and Weaver parking lot.

Emrys sat on the steps.

"You want me to beat him up?" Rouge asked.

"No," Nathan said. "Just go in. I'll handle that."

They exited the car.

Robin held back.

Rouge blanked Emrys as he walked to the door.

Nathan walked up to him. "I just think you should know before you open your mouth, Oban got her memory back. She told me everything."

"I know," Emrys said so low it was hard to hear. "He said as much when he and and the others arrived."

"Why are you here?"

Emrys stood up. "I know this is the last thing you want to hear from me, but I understand why you felt betrayed. I just wanted to say, I am sorry. I should have told you."

"Yes," Nathan said, "You were hired by the man who ruined my life to kill me. Don't you think I would want to know that?"

"How was I supposed to bring it up?"

"I don't know. Maybe, one day while we were getting dolled up you might have said something like, O, everyone, just so you know, I am a contract killer."

Emrys looked away. "I'm not. Paul sought me out. I am a lot older than I look, and I was bored. It sounded interesting."

"Murder sounded interesting?" Nathan took a step back.

"While it doesn't justify it, you need to know you are the first person I ever cared for."

"That makes it better?"

Emrys huffed.

"Why me? What was special about me?"

"I was distracted by your innocence, your spirit. You believe so much. To be honest, I drank my own poison for you."

"What?"

"I don't know how to explain it to you without sounding worse. I am a monster."

"I can tell."

Emrys shook all over, "It doesn't make it right, but I was born this way. I am a cambion. I was bred to be a monster."

Nathan saw something in Emrys that broke his heart. "My God, you were, weren't you?"

Nodding, Emrys looked up through tears.

He didn't want to forgive him, but he started wondering if it was better to keep him at Wand and Weaver than to release him into the wild.

"What if I asked you to stay?" Nathan asked.

Emrys grabbed his chest. "Would you consider that?"

"Answer my question first."

"I love you, Nathan. I will always love you. There is literally nothing either one of us can do to change that. If you asked me to stay, I would stay. I won't push myself on you. I will do whatever you ask."

Nathan thought about it. Part of him never wanted to see Emrys again.

"You're not thinking of kicking him out, are you?" Robin called out from behind him.

"Emrys," The words were so hard to say, "Please stay."

Robin watched Nathan and Emrys walk into Wand and Weaver.

He heard slow clapping behind him.

"Hello, Jack," Robin sighed. He walked toward the door.

"Aw," Jack said. "You don't want to stay here and chat?" Robin didn't look back. He opened the door and walked around the bar to set up.

Jack walked in right behind him.

"We're not open. Get out."

"Nah," Jack stood in front of the bar. "I think we need to talk."

"I'm done with you, Jack. Why won't you please leave me alone?"

"Your beloved Nathan took the cambion back. Surely you can take a moment for me."

Robin started his prep work. He hoped he looked menacing working with the knife as he cut his citrus, and other garnishes.

"You are lucky you're not wearing black today. Nathan is a lucky boy."

Jack slapped his palms on the bar.

Robin didn't react.

"Well, to business then. I have convinced Titania to call you back. After what Nathan did, he is obviously a danger to us all."

"What did he do?"

"Didn't he tell you? Oh, maybe he didn't know." Jack laughed.

Robin felt a rope tighten around him. He closed his eyes. He knew Jack was trying to wrap him in a fae web. He rooted his feet into the floor.

Jack pulled.

Robin didn't move. He extended a heart chain to the bar. He locked the fetters tight.

Jack scowled at him, but broke into smile. "This could have been easier."

"No, it really couldn't."

Jack stormed out of the bar.

Robin went back to his prep. He was afraid of what Jack was planning.

When they opened the doors, he was happy to see so many people pour in. Their little publicity storm yesterday seemed to work.

He couldn't get Jack out of his mind. He was plotting something big. He had to be ready for whatever he was planning.

The crowd was energetic, and overflowing with love for the fetehouse. He knew what he had to do.

Leaving the bar, Robin relaxed into his nature. His skin took on a soft glow. He reached out to the sound system and chose the song that had to be on.

He leapt onto the stage as the haunting chorus and horns introduced Within Temptation's Jillian.

Light bubbled from his back into luminous dragonfly wings.

He replaced the lead vocals with his own. His voice resonated in the rafters and filled the room.

On the chorus, he opened his heart. Light burst from his chest hiding strands of fate and destiny.

As he sang, the crowd swayed. Their affection rose like tall savanna grass. They loved him. They connected with the words and the emotion, the hope and the fear. Their strands waved across the room.

On the second chorus, he grasped them in his hands.

A choir of hooded fey illusions walked out from behind him at the chorus. He bound the strands together and wrapped them as a rope around his waist.

Mist fell from them onto the stage, scintillating like a starry field.

Robin dropped into the field, through the floor and erupted again at the final chorus wearing the stars like a luxurious, draping robe.

He spun, tossing the sea of stars around him like a galaxy of his own design.

The song ended, Robin released the stars in a furious shower and landed on the stage. The chain was tight.

Nathan joined the thunderous applause. He didn't know Robin could sing or he would have asked him to perform before. The applause quieted.

Robin hopped off the stage. Nathan clasped hands with him and slapped him on the back.

"That was amazing," Nathan said.

"You have no idea."

Thunder!

The door ripped off its hinges and flew across the room.

The Dwayyo lunged through the opening into the bar.

Screams filled the air.

The crowd rushed toward the stage. No one took their eyes off the beast.

Emrys and Daniel stepped forward.

"Get back," Nathan yelled.

The wolf-man walked further into the room and howled.

Nathan took a step in front of the others. "Get out of our house!"

The crowd roared.

The beast looked at them with a savage intelligence working behind those amber eyes. It stepped towards them.

Emrys pushed Nathan back. "Am I going to have to hurt you again?" Emrys asked. "The swarm is already on its way."

Nathan almost fell down.

The wolf-man pointed at Robin, and snarled.

"Emrys," Robin said, "You don't know who you're up against."

"I'm not stupid," Emrys winked at the beast, "Get out."

The wolf tried to step around him.

Emrys moved into his way. He flared his arms out at his side and stared the creature in the eye. Shadows flowed like a fog off his arms.

The beast stepped to the right, and pressed forward.

Emrys was already there. He raised his arms and a wall of shadows rose between the crowd and him.

"If your mother wants blood, take mine," Emrys said, "I have not had all my choices taken away from me, only to let you take Robin's choice from him."

Nathan couldn't understand what he was seeing. After all he learned about Emrys, it just didn't make sense. Was he looking for redemption, or was he just itching for a fight.

The dance went back and forth a couple times. The beast moved, and Emrys blocked it.

The creature snarled with rage, and looked down on Emrys. He looked so small and fragile next to the towering silver furred monster.

The beast snarled. "Why do you care, cambion?" The wolf growled. Its voice was wild and tonal, rough and violent.

The crowd screeched and pressed back against the stage.

"Because," Emrys stood his ground and looked up in the wolf's gleaming maw, "Everyone deserves their own life."

The beast narrowed its eyes, and sniffed the air. He stepped up to Emrys, and loomed over him. He bore his teeth. Flattening his ears against his neck, He snarled down at Emrys. "Would you give up your life for a fae?" He put his razor sharp claws to Emrys' throat.

Emrys didn't move.

The air was so thin, it was hard to breathe.

Emrys stood there like a statue. He didn't flinch, didn't blink. The beast's breath blew his hair away from his face.

"Trust," The wolf snorted. He released a single belly laugh that shook the floor and walls.

He pulled back his clawed hand and looked up at Robin. His eyes were cold and curious. He nodded so sharp and fast some of the patrons thought he was about to charge. Instead, he turned around. He walked toward the door.

As he walked away, light dripped off of his shoulders and head. He shrank a little with each step from nine feet to over six. His muscles rippled as the fur melted away into golden strands of light that drifted off into the air before dissolving into nothing. A black suit materialized on his back. His silver hair atop his head shortened.

"Sorry about the mess," his refined genteel voice rang out.

As he walked out the door, he reached a single white hand behind him, twisting like he grabbed a table cloth and pulled it from a table. The door returned to its place.

www.ingramcontent.com/pod-product-compliance
Lightning Source LLC
Chambersburg PA
CBHW061248280526
45784CB00002B/678